The Countryside Companion

Compiled by Dennis and Jan Kelsall

CONTENTS

ACKNOWLEDGEMENTS

Text:	Dennis and Jan Kelsall
Photography:	DK – Dennis and Jan Kelsall
	MR – Mike Read, www.mikeread.co.uk
	IS – iStockphoto
	SFI – Stock Free Images
	KF – Kevin Freeborn
Design:	Ark Creative (UK) Ltd

© Crimson Publishing Ltd

This edition first published in Great Britain 2013 by
Crimson Publishing, Westminster House, Kew Road,
Richmond, Surrey, TW9 2ND

The right of Dennis and Jan Kelsall to be identified as the authors
of this work has been asserted by them in accordance with the
Copyright, Designs and Patents Act, 1988.

While every care has been taken to check the accuracy and reliability
of the information in this guide, the authors and publisher cannot
accept responsibility for errors or omissions or for changes in details
given. When walking in the countryside it is advisable at all times
to act with due care and attention, and to observe the law and the
Countryside Code.

ISBN: 978-1-78059-110-0

Printed in Singapore. 1/13

A catalogue record for this book is available from the British Library.

Front cover: Highland cattle; orange tip; stepping stones over the
River Ure; Brent goose
Back cover: Barn owl on a footpath fingerpost

There was a time when people's lives were intimately linked to the countryside; most lived in small villages and depended upon the land for their livelihood. The majority of us in 21st-century Britain inhabit towns and cities, and although increasingly we head to the countryside for recreation, familiarity has faded. Today's generation is losing the ability to recognise the plants, birds and animals that our grandparents took for granted.

This guide is an ideal companion for your country rambles. A packed introduction to the amazing diversity and richness of the British countryside, it provides a beautifully illustrated reference of things to spot and identify when you are out and about. Walk with senses alert and the pleasurable rewards of doing so will be many: the sight in spring of tiny hedge bank violets, the sound of a woodpecker drumming and the smell of wild garlic. The Countryside Companion will enrich your walks, introducing you to a variety of landscapes and an array of the commoner species and other features you might encounter along the way.

Armed with this guide you should be able to recognise more than 450 different species of wildlife and aspects of the countryside from clouds to dovecotes and Jersey cows to Scots pine. Britain has so much to offer that this guide can only scratch the surface. But once able to recognise these, there is a wealth of more specialist identification guides on the market to deepen your interest.

Get more from your walks The countryside is always changing, so get more from your walks by visiting a route at a different time of day, in another season or by reversing the direction of travel. You will be more successful at seeing birds and mammals by walking quietly and slowly. Take regular pauses and let the wildlife come to you. Early morning or late evening is often the best time to spot shyer creatures. Walking within the protected environment of a national or local nature reserve will also increase your chances of a successful wildlife encounter.

Rivington Country Park, Lancashire

It pays to plan the day. Choose a route within the capacity of the group, taking into account distance, terrain and weather. Study local weather forecasts and note sunset time.

What to wear British weather is changeable and you should be prepared. Ideally, wear comfortable, waterproof walking boots offering good ankle support and grip. Quality socks are equally important. For the body, several thin layers are preferable to a bulky sweater. A synthetic base layer helps wick away perspiration while insulating mid layers such as a fleece give warmth. The best waterproof outer layers are of breathable fabrics. Gaiters help deflect snow, water and mud from your boots and offer protection against undergrowth. For the same reason, shorts are not always sensible in summer.

What to take Select a comfortable rucksack. Essential gear includes a first aid kit, torch and whistle. In the hills, a survival bag can be a life-saver. Many people find walking poles helpful in distributing weight and maintaining balance. Beyond that, a small camera and binoculars are useful. Remember your mobile phone, but be aware that coverage is extremely patchy in country areas.

Drinking enough is always a problem; recommendations suggest 2 litres per day, but in warm weather or at altitude, even this is not enough. Take a hot drink or water and avoid aerated drinks and alcohol.

Even if planning lunch at a pub or café (check opening times beforehand), it is wise to carry emergency rations such as raisins, nuts and energy bars; alternatively pack sandwiches or pies.

Staying safe Remember mountain and winter walking demands skill, experience and equipment. Basic factors to consider are wind chill and the drop of temperature with altitude. When scrambling, remember that it is always easier to climb up than get back down - never over-estimate your ability.

Tell someone where you are going and when you expect to finish, particularly if venturing alone and remember to notify them of your return. Should the terrain be more difficult than anticipated, the weather deteriorate or you become tired, consider turning back or choosing an alternate route.

When walking on roads face oncoming traffic and take especial care on blind bends. Look and listen carefully when crossing railway tracks, high-speed trains can be surprisingly quiet.

Beware of the bull! Unless aggravated, livestock are rarely a problem, but maintain a sensible distance and avoid getting between a cow and her calf. Although cattle can be inquisitive, they are usually deterred if faced with outstretched arms.

Walking with a dog This brings its own responsibilities; it too can get tired, be affected by the weather and find difficulty with stiles. They should be kept under control, particularly passing other walkers. Most reported attacks by farm animals involve a dog, so keep your dog on a short lead. If livestock do become aggressive, remain calm, let the dog free and leave by the nearest exit. Remove dog waste for disposal in an appropriate bin.

Highland cattle across the path near Ripponden, Calderdale

Exploring the countryside

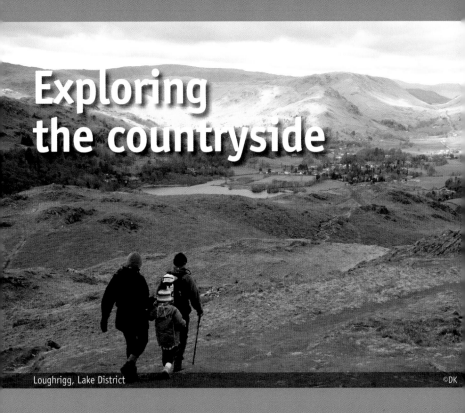

Loughrigg, Lake District ©DK

The British Isles is an extensive archipelago numbering more than 1,000 islands that vary in size from Ireland to Bishop's Rock, a desolate wave-swept reef off the Scilly Isles hardly big enough to accommodate its lighthouse. Barely 600 miles from top to bottom, the mainland encompasses an area of around 88,750 square miles, enclosed within a coastline that runs for some 7,700 miles, about one-third of the Earth's circumference. Yet surprisingly, nowhere is more than 70 miles from the sea. According to the Ordnance Survey, Church Flatts Farm near Coton in the Elms in Derbyshire is Britain's most inland point.

Britain has one of the most diverse but compact landscapes in the world, laid out on a scale that is both intimate and accessible. Distinctive landscape types range from mountainous semi-tundra to coastal marsh, karst plateaux and gorges to rolling downs, and forest to arable farmland. With up to 180 inches (450mm) of annual rainfall, Snowdonia and the Lake District are two of the wettest places in Europe, yet only 200 miles away parts of East Anglia are drier than Beirut. Average annual temperatures lie between a moderate 8.5°C and 11°C, but the mercury has plummeted to −27°C in the Scottish Highlands and risen to 38.5°C in Kent. Wind speeds of up to 170mph have been recorded on top of Cairn Gorm, while down in Eastbourne, the monthly sunshine percentage has equalled that of Nice.

Now approaching 61 million, Britain ranks high in the world's population density table, but with 90% of people living in an urban environment, there are large areas of rural countryside, wild coastline and open upland where habitation is scattered and the landscape largely unspoiled. More than a quarter of Britain is protected within 15 National Parks, 42 AONBs (England and Wales) and 40 National Scenic Areas (Scotland). Also, thousands of nature reserves and other protected sites dotted up and down the country, around the coast and even offshore provide important habitats for wildlife.

WHERE YOU CAN WALK

Virtually all land is owned by someone, but much is accessible on foot using Access Land, public rights of way and permissive paths.

ACCESS LAND ▶

In England and Wales, you can (subject to restriction) wander at will across Access Land, tinted as such upon Ordnance Survey Explorer/Outdoor Leisure maps.

- Access Land (shown by a pale yellow tint)
- Access information point
- Access Land in a wooded area (shown by a bright green tint)
- Access Land boundary

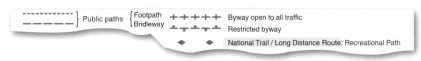

Public paths { Footpath / Bridleway }   +++++ Byway open to all traffic
⊥⊤⊥⊤⊥⊤ Restricted byway
◆ ◆ National Trail / Long Distance Route; Recreational Path

----------- Permitted Path
----------- } Permitted Bridleway

▲ PERMISSIVE PATHS

These are concessionary paths and bridleways negotiated with the land owner; they are not rights of way. Because they are permissive, they can be closed. Many waterside towpaths are permissive paths. More information can be obtained from local authorities and the Natural England website. In addition, many estate owners, including the National Trust, water utility companies and the Forestry Commission, have opened permissive paths across their land. Marked as orange pecked or dashed lines, these may be shown on Ordnance Survey Explorer/Outdoor Leisure maps.

PUBLIC RIGHTS OF WAY ▲

Public footpaths, bridleways and byways, generally signed from the road, lead across otherwise private land. These are shown as dark green pecked or dashed lines on Ordnance Survey Explorer/Outdoor Leisure maps.

SCOTLAND

In Scotland, the position is different, since walkers have enjoyed traditional access to much of the countryside. Although few rights of way are recorded on Scottish maps, you can follow most paths and tracks or wander responsibly across open land. There are common sense exclusions, which are detailed in the Scottish Outdoor Access Code. During the deer stalking season (usually between 1 July and 20 October), the Hillphones service gives information as to where shoots are taking place.

Not everything, however, that is clearly marked on the map is as obvious on the ground. Infrequently walked routes across crop fields, pastures and open country may be totally unapparent or at best defined by a vague trod. A good sense of direction, an ability to read the ground (skills that develop with experience) and attention to the map then become necessary. *Where paths are faint, especially over moor or mountainside, do not walk in misty or poor weather unless experienced in such conditions and able to navigate by map and compass.*

Britain has more than 150,000 miles of off-road rights of way and a plethora of tracks, trods and permissive paths to which the walker has access. Many follow traditional routes, droves and old roads ignored by the modern network; others were simply local paths between farms, villages, churches and workplaces.

PREHISTORIC ROUTES ▶

The genesis of today's network lies in prehistoric trackways that connected trade and ceremonial centres. The Ridgeway National Trail follows much of the original ancient chalk ridge route running between Overton Hill in Wiltshire and Ivinghoe Beacon in Buckinghamshire. It is one of the oldest, continuously used pathways in Britain. The discovery of timber causeways such as the Sweet Track (3800BC) on the Somerset Levels indicates that low-lying routes are equally old.

On The Ridgeway towards Ivinghoe Beacon

DROVE ROADS ▼

At one time cattle and other livestock, including geese, were walked between seasonal pastures or to market along drove roads. Left wide to accommodate large herds, they avoided villages and can be recognised in some of today's broad-verged lanes and tracks.

Wheeldale Moor, North York Moors

ROMAN ROADS ▲

The Romans built over 10,000 miles of stone-paved roads. However, most were subsequently abandoned and throughout the Dark and Middle Ages there was just a sparse network of rough tracks linking towns and monasteries. Paved roads only reappeared in the 18th century with the development of the turnpikes, but it took the motorcar to generate today's 245,000 miles of road.

Near Bourton-on-the-Water, Cotswolds

PACKHORSE ROUTES ▼

During the Middle Ages, few roads were capable of supporting wheeled traffic and most goods were carried on pack animals. Packhorse routes were the arteries of trade, but unlike the droves, they were narrow, for the horses travelled in single file.

CAUSEYS ▼

On poor ground, paths were occasionally paved with stone slabs and known as causeys. They are notably found in the Yorkshire Dales where they snake across meadows linking villages, mines and quarries. Causeys are again being laid in some places to help protect the peat from erosion.

Near Dove Head, Peak District

Great Hill, Lancashire ©DK

Maps, compass, GPS and route descriptions are invaluable in keeping you to your intended path, but there are plenty of aids dotted around the countryside to assist in route finding including fingerposts, waymarks and milestones.

FINGERPOSTS ▶

Confidently pointing the way along a lane, across a field, through woodland or over desolate moor, fingerposts can name the destination, give its distance (in miles, kilometres or time) or simply identify the line of the path, written as 'Llwybr Cyhoeddus' in Welsh.

WAYMARKS ▼

In England and Wales, coloured waymarks identify different types of rights of way. Yellow arrows indicate footpaths and blue arrows denote bridleways, which can be used by horse riders and cyclists as well. Byways are marked with plum-coloured or red arrows, which indicate whether they are restricted or not, that is, open to vehicles. In Scotland, lowland paths may be waymarked, but as a rule, hill paths are unmarked.

Salthouse, Norfolk

WAYMARKED ROUTES ▼

There are more than 700 other routes documented by the Long Distance Walkers' Association as well as countless lesser routes devised by local authorities, the Forestry Commission, National Trust and ramblers' groups. Identified by distinctive and often quirky motifs, they frequently follow historical, geographical or naturalist themes and explore some of the best countryside within the local area.

NATIONAL TRAILS ▶

There are presently 19 National Trails, managed by the Countryside Agency, Scottish Natural Heritage or Countryside Council for Wales and which pass through some of Britain's most dramatic, wildest and beautiful scenery. In England and Wales they are marked with a distinctive acorn symbol while in Scotland trails carry a thistle logo.

National Trail acorn waymark

CROSSES ▶

Throughout history crosses were erected across the countryside to mark a crossing of paths or tracks. Occasionally they simply give reassurance in a lonely place that a traveller was on the right track. Many survive, famously those on the North York Moors, where Ralph's Cross is used as the National Park's symbol.

MILESTONES ▼

Like roads, milestones came to Britain with the Romans, spaced at intervals of a Roman mile (about 1,600 yards). Most survivors are now in museums but an example can be seen near Vindolanda in Northumberland. Milestones reappeared with the turnpikes and canals in the 18th century. Although the mile was standardised in 1592, local variations persisted into the 19th century, sometimes extending to 3,300 yards.

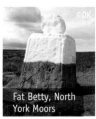

Fat Betty, North York Moors

Bride Stones Moor, Calderdale

CAIRNS ▲

Cairns or piles of stones line many footpaths, particularly in hill and moorland areas. They may serve to confirm the line of the path, mark a junction or the summit of a peak. Most are crude heaps varying from a handful of pebbles to monumental piles that emulate the cairns marking prehistoric burials. Some, however, are crafted with great precision and stand as intriguing tall columns upon a bleak landscape. They occasionally appear in groups known as 'stone men' such as those on Wild Boar Fell, Cumbria (pictured).

Aire and Calder Navigation milestone, Hebden Bridge, Calderdale

◀ TRIG POINTS

Often simply referred to as 'trigs', these concrete columns grace many of the country's mountains and hills. However, they do not always mark the summit; indeed the lowest stands one metre below sea level near Little Ouse in Cambridgeshire. The pillars were constructed during the re-triangulation of Britain by Ordnance Survey, which began in 1935 and was completed 27 years later, defining the National Grid system. Every pillar was placed to give a line of site to at least two others and careful determination of the angles between each enabled the triangulation nationwide to an accuracy of 20 metres. GPS measurements give a precision better than one metre over the same distance, making most triangulation columns redundant.

Pendle Hill, Lancashire

BOUNDARIES AND CROSSINGS

Marked with a fine, solid black line on OS maps, field and road boundaries may be walls, hedges or fences. In fenland, drainage ditches serve the same purpose and are shown as a thin blue line.

BOUNDARY MARKERS ▶

You may encounter old boundary stones indicating land ownership, while truly ancient territorial boundaries, such as Bokerley Ditch (Dorset) or Hadrian's Wall (northern England) remain impressively visible, snaking over many miles. Subtler are prehistoric field boundaries in the form of upright slabs of stone, such as those above Grassington in the Yorkshire Dales.

Where path and boundary intersect, there is often a gate or stile. Confusingly, particularly in the north, gate can also refer to the path itself, such as Doctor's Gate near Glossop or Withens Gate near Todmorden.

Boundary stone near Ripponden, Calderdale

Hadrian's Wall, Walltown Crags, Northumberland

BANKS, DRY STONE WALLS AND HEDGES ▼

Medieval fields were generally vast, divided into 'strips' for cultivation by individual villagers with livestock being grazed on open commons or hillsides. Significant enclosure began during the 15th century and continued into the 19th century, boundaries being constructed of earth bank, dry stone wall or hedge. In the Yorkshire Dales alone there are some 5,500 miles of stone walling. Walling displays regional variations as does hedge laying, dependent upon its purpose. Hedges and dry stone walls are havens for wildflowers and wildlife and the variety and type of species in a hedge give clues to its age.

GATES ▼

Wide enough to accommodate tractors or stock, field gates range from traditional five-bar gates to the now little-used field stile or stoup, where rather than being hinged, the gate has projecting wooden rails that slot into grooved gate posts. Pedestrian gates are generally styled on a bar gate, whereas pickets have vertical slats. A wicket is a small gate or door generally set within a larger one. Unlatched gates can allow animals to stray, but the kissing-gate controls passage through a small intermediate enclosure. Occasionally a wall gap is narrowed to dispense with the need for a gate and becomes known as a squeeze-gap, passage sometimes further complicated by the inclusion of a post in the centre.

Kissing-gate

Milldale, Peak District

A laid hedge near Killington, Cumbria

STILES ▶

Stiles have to be climbed and usually take the form of wooden or stone steps rising either side of the barrier. Ladder stiles are used for higher boundaries and may be 10 feet tall to surmount a deer fence. Variations are limited only by the ingenuity of the builder and can combine features of gate, stile and squeeze gap within a single structure.

Near Austwick, Yorkshire Dales

Near Lambutts, Calderdale

Barbondale, Yorkshire

STEPPING STONES ▼

Stepping stones on the other hand enabled a dry-shod crossing and were sometimes associated with monastic routes. The most basic consisted of a single sturdy boulder set in the middle of the stream. Wider streams, rivers and even muddy estuaries used stones set at intervals and had the advantage over bridges of being able to survive a flood.

FORDS ▲

Fords involve getting your feet (or more) wet and were once widespread. Locations are preserved in place names – Oxford, Abbotsford, Salford and less obviously, Stainforth near Settle (stony ford) or Handforth in Cheshire (Hanna's ford). They were often located by a bend where slowing water creates shallows and the lowest fording point of a river frequently grew to an important town.

River Ure, Yorkshire Dales

BRIDGES ▼

The earliest surviving bridges, known as clapper bridges, are prehistoric. At their simplest, they consist of a single slab of rock between the two banks. Wider crossings could be achieved by using intermediate piers to create a causeway. The longest is Tarr Steps on Exmoor with 17 spans.

Clapper bridge, Malham, Yorkshire Dales

Landscape features

Hilbre Island, Wirral   ©DK

The Earth is around 4.6 billion years old and tectonic movement, volcanism, periodic flooding, deposition and erosion have all contributed to the shaping of its face. However, only during the last 600 million years has the land we know as Britain come together while drifting north from below the Equator. Indeed, its separation from continental Europe occurred just a geological eye-blink ago at the end of the last glacial period.

The geology of an area determines its character, influencing everything from topography and the flora and fauna to vernacular architecture. Fundamental is the underlying rock, of which there are three distinct types.

Igneous rocks are solidified magma, the molten material that lies beneath the Earth's crust. Lava ejected from volcanic eruption cooled quickly to produce fine crystalline rocks such as the basalt surrounding Fingal's Cave on Staffa. Extrusions cooling slowly beneath the surface, on the other hand, form coarse-grained rocks like the granite tors outcropping on Dartmoor or forming the core of many of Scotland's high mountains.

Sedimentary rocks are the compacted accumulation of debris. Silt and sand settling beneath water formed shale and sandstone, whereas pebbles and gravel deposited along ancient seashores, estuaries or river beds produced conglomerates. Plant matter accumulating in swamps became coal, while limestone is the calcareous accretion of tiny creatures beneath shallow seas, chalk being a particularly pure form. Fossils most commonly occur in sedimentary rocks and are the petrified remains of animal and plant life. The Jurassic limestones and mudstones of the south Devon and Dorset coast are particularly rich in fossilised remains.

Metamorphic rocks can originate from either of the above, but have been subsequently altered by pressure, heat and chemical action. Marbles and the slates of Wales and the northern Lake District are typical examples. The Gneiss found in north-west Scotland is also metamorphic and, at some 2.7 billion years is the oldest rock in Britain.

At its peak in Britain, some 20,000 years ago, **glaciers** originating in the mountains through snow accumulation over many years, spawned **ice sheets** that were more than 1 mile thick, and which radiated across the surrounding lowland and seas as far south as the River Thames and the Bristol Channel. They altered the landscape in three dramatic ways; erosion – wearing away the soil and bedrock, transportation – carrying the debris within the ice, and deposition – dumping it, often many miles from is origin.

U-SHAPED VALLEY ▷

Glaciers developed along pre-existing drainage patterns, dramatically deepening and widening them to leave valleys that are typically steep-sided, flat-bottomed and often straight – the 'U' shaped valley. Fine examples are to be found throughout Snowdonia, the Lake District and the Scottish Highlands.

Langdale, Lake District

Glen Etive, Highland

CORRIE ▽

A corrie or cwm is a cauldron-like amphitheatre high on a mountain and was the starting point of a glacier. Over time, accumulating snow compacted as glacial ice and eventually began moving downhill, enlarging the hollow by plucking rock from its back and sides.

Cairngorms National Park, Highland

TARN and LOCHAN △

Many corries now contain small lakes or tarns, lochans in Scotland, the water filling an over-deepened hollow or held back by the debris of a recessional moraine. Lacking in nutrients, they are often bare of plant life.

◁ PYRAMIDAL PEAK and ARÊTE

An arête is a knife-edge ridge created by glacial erosion along two adjacent valleys, such as Helvelyn's Striding Edge in the Lake District. A similar formation occurs between two corries or valley heads that have eaten backwards into the mountain from different sides. Erosion in three or more corries can create a pyramidal peak, a true mountain summit such as Buachaille Etive Mor in Glen Coe.

HANGING VALLEY ▽

Being smaller, tributary glaciers deepen at a considerably lesser rate than the principal flow. When the ice retreats these tributary valleys are left 'hanging' high on the side of the main valley, their streams cascading in waterfalls. The Grey Mare's Tail drops 200 feet at the head of Moffat Dale and Cautley Spout in the Howgills are spectacular examples.

Aber Falls, Snowdonia

FEATURES CREATED BY ICE

Goat's Water, Lake District
©SFI

SCREE ▲

Although the glaciers have long gone, the freeze-thaw action of frost over countless winters continues to erode mountainsides. The shattered rock debris accumulates below exposed rock slopes as scree.

MORAINE ▶

Moraines are an accumulation of debris carried and deposited by a glacier. Lateral moraines are parallel ridges along the valley, whereas terminal moraines lie across a valley formed at the glacier's snout. Recessional moraines indicate pauses during a glacier's retreat, sometimes impounding a series of lakes, although many subsequently drained to leave a series of shallow steps along the valley. Moraine deposits can be found in the Cairngorm glens and Lake District valleys.

A pingo pond, Thompson Common, Norfolk
©DK

PINGO ▲

Ponds and meres might have glacial origins, like those of Cheshire and the pingos of Norfolk. 'Pingo' is an Innuit word meaning 'small hill'. They formed under permafrost conditions where ice within the frozen ground pushed the overlying earth into mounds. During periods of thawing in the permafrost's upper layers, soil slips would build up a ring of debris. When the permafrost melted lipped craters remained, filling with water to give the pools seen today.

ERRATIC ▼

Ice sheets can transport rock and debris many miles from their origin. Sand and gravel is termed glacial till, but larger rocks and boulders are known as erratics. In the Yorkshire Dales, the Norber boulders (pictured) are sandstone and have been carried uphill from nearby Crummockdale to be abandoned on a limestone slope. The 2,000 ton Bowder Stone in Borrowdale (Lake District) had its origins in Scotland.

©DK

Wrynose Pass, Lake District
©MR

RIBBON LAKE ▼

Ribbon lakes are long bodies of water occurring in glacial valleys. They may be held back by terminal or recessional moraines. Alternatively, where the valley floor has alternating soft and harder rock, the glacier erodes more deeply into the soft rock leaving a raised lip when encountering the more resistant rock, which then acts as a dam to create a lake. Windermere (Lake District) is a typical example and at 10½ miles long is England's largest lake.

Loch Arklet, The Trossachs
©DK

Rivers exhibit an ever-changing character throughout their course. Surface runoff coalesces into streams, which in upland areas tend to be fast-flowing – too swift to allow rooting plants. Mature flows and lowland rivers like the Thames are slower but nutrient-rich, the shallows thick with underwater plants. Britain's longest river is the Severn, 220 miles from the Ceredigion Hills to the Bristol Channel.

RIVER VALLEY ▼

Ice dams and post glacial rivers had many dramatic effects. Everywhere are valleys disproportional to their present streams, their dramatic contours created by the deluging meltwater. The Peak District's limestone gorges impressively illustrate this. Ice altered the course of many rivers and occasionally reversed the flow; the Derwent once ran east through the Vale of Pickering to debouche at Filey.

Lathkill Dale, Peak District

River Wye near Chepstow

RIVER MEANDER ▲

The power of slow-moving flood plain rivers derives from their volume and the gradual erosion of the outer bank at a bend can eventually result in the river developing an ever-more pronounced meander. The Cuckmere in East Sussex is a wonderful example. In time, however, the river might breach the neck of the meander and in straightening its course, the old meander is left as an oxbow lake.

GORGE and WATERFALL ▼

Hard bedrock is relatively resistant to erosion, but where a fast-flowing river then meets softer substrata a waterfall can develop. The weaker rock is worn away more quickly to produce a deepening gorge downstream, while the turbulent power of the cascading water can erode the base of the underlying rock. In time the unsupported lip collapses and the waterfall retreats upstream as at High Force in upper Teesdale.

Hardraw Force, Yorkshire Dales

RIVER CLIFF

The erosive power of a river is greatest against the outer flank of a bend, enabling it to under-cut the bank forming a river cliff. The height might be anything from a few feet upwards; those overlooking the River Wye above Chepstow being particularly spectacular.

SINK HOLES ▼

Limestone is slightly soluble in the weak acidity of rainwater. In areas of carboniferous limestone in the Mendips, the Peak District, Yorkshire Dales and central Scotland, disappearing streams and dry valleys are characteristic. Cavernous mouths of potholes, deep gorges and swallet holes are surface features of extensive underground cave systems, created by the corrosive action of water over millennia.

Hunt Pot, Ribblesdale, Yorkshire Dales

COASTAL FEATURES

Britain's most varied and naturally changing environment is where land and sea meet.

CLIFFS ▶

Coastal cliffs provide Britain's most dramatic seaside scenery; the tallest on the mainland are in north Devon rising to over 1,000 feet. Pounding waves, sea currents and the tide's bi-diurnal ebb and flow combine to wear away cliffs. The resistance of the cliff face rock to erosion determines the rate of retreat. Parts of East Yorkshire's North Sea coastline suffer the fastest rate of erosion in Europe, retreating about five feet per year.

Fast-retreating cliffs at East Runton, Norfolk

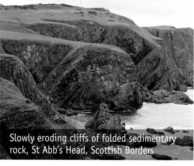

Slowly eroding cliffs of folded sedimentary rock, St Abb's Head, Scottish Borders

◀ STACKS

Incessant wave action attacks the base of cliffs, exploiting faults and softer rock to create coves and natural arches. Lulworth Cove and Durdle Door on Dorset's Jurassic Coast are particularly fine examples. Stacks, such as Old Harry, are remnants that have become detached from the main cliff.

Old Harry Rocks, near Swanage, Dorset

RAISED BEACH ▼

Along Britain's west coast, particularly western Scotland, the land has risen, rebounding from the ice cover of the last glacial period and leaving former cliffs and shorelines well above present-day beaches; classic raised beaches can be seen at Port-Eynon (pictured) and the Bile near Portree, Skye.

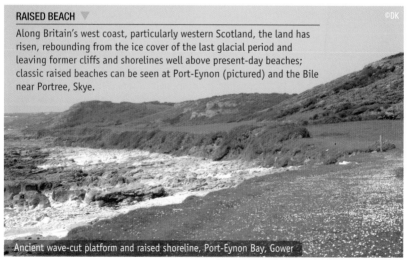

Ancient wave-cut platform and raised shoreline, Port-Eynon Bay, Gower

INTER-TIDAL ZONE ▼

One of the most rewarding places to wander is along the inter-tidal zone, where flotsam and shells are washed on to the beach and low tide exposes pools on a rocky shore. Scallop, whelk and razor shells are amongst those commonly found, rarer is the delicate shell of a sand urchin. Starfish and jellyfish may be washed up by the tide together with bundles of kelp dislodged from deeper water by storm waves. Mussels and limpets cling to the rocks while in the pools, particularly harsh places to live since evaporating water creates high levels of salinity, are prawns, shrimps and anemones.

©DK

You may also find shore crabs, its body squarer than the edible crab (pictured) or perhaps a hermit crab wearing the discarded shell of a whelk.

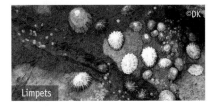
©DK
Limpets

©DK
Nicholstan Burrows. Oxwich Bay, Gower

DUNE COAST ▲

Extensive beaches backed by low-lying land can give rise to dunes, the gradual accumulation of wind-blown sand forming a sweep of shifting hills, such as those found at Formby, Lancashire. Dune plants are highly specialised and vital for stabilisation, for without their binding roots the sand would just as easily disperse. Plants like marram grass and sea rocket have leaves evolved to reduce moisture loss and deep roots to tap groundwater.

©DK
Drowned glacial valley, Loch Long, Argyll and Bute

DROWNED COASTAL VALLEYS ▲

Milford Haven, Southampton Water and Plymouth Sound are flooded river estuaries, termed rias, while many Scottish sea lochs are submerged, over-deepened glacial valleys.

ESTUARINE COAST ▼

Revealed at low tide, the extensive mudflats and salt marshes such as those of the Essex coast, Chichester Harbour (West Sussex) and the Ribble estuary (Lancashire) are rich in molluscs, worms and crustaceans and are favoured feeding grounds for many birds. Dunlin and redshank are amongst the waders that probe the mud with long beaks, while pink-footed and Brent geese overwinter on the tidal flats. Plant life too is specialised, long roots helping to stabilise the silt: glasswort (once used in the production of glass – pictured, foreground), seablite and sea aster can tolerate high salt levels.

©DK
Dingle Marshes, Dunwich, Suffolk

Hookney Tor, Dartmoor, Devon ©MR

MOORLAND

Moorlands are upland areas with poor, acidic soils. Having a generally cool, wet climate, the ground can often be waterlogged, leaving a deforested wilderness that provides at best poor grazing for hardy sheep. Much of Exmoor, Dartmoor, the Welsh hills and the Pennines are covered by acidic peat (slowly decaying plant matter), which, despite accumulating at less than half inch in ten years, often lies to great depths. Bilberry is a moorland shrub whose tiny fruit makes delicious eating.

Bilberry ©DK

Sutton Heath, Suffolk

©MR

HEATHLAND

Although cloaked in heather and superficially similar to moorland, heath is a lowland landscape founded on sandy soils rather than peat. The Egdon Heath of Thomas Hardy's novels once spread across Dorset, and the Norfolk brecklands were extensive. Southern England has 20% of the world's heathland, managed by light grazing to conserve this internationally rare environment. The Dartford warbler is only found on heathland.

Dartford warbler

©DK

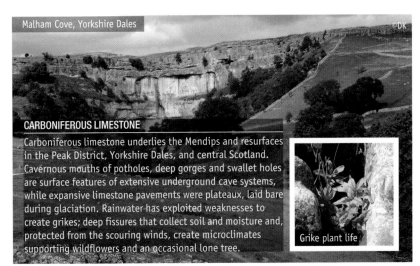
Malham Cove, Yorkshire Dales
©DK

CARBONIFEROUS LIMESTONE

Carboniferous limestone underlies the Mendips and resurfaces in the Peak District, Yorkshire Dales, and central Scotland. Cavernous mouths of potholes, deep gorges and swallet holes are surface features of extensive underground cave systems, while expansive limestone pavements were plateaux, laid bare during glaciation. Rainwater has exploited weaknesses to create grikes; deep fissures that collect soil and moisture and, protected from the scouring winds, create microclimates supporting wildflowers and an occasional lone tree.

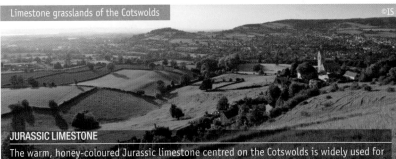
Grike plant life

Limestone grasslands of the Cotswolds
©IS

JURASSIC LIMESTONE

The warm, honey-coloured Jurassic limestone centred on the Cotswolds is widely used for building, bringing character to Bath and Cheltenham and manifested in the numerous quintessential English villages that lie in the gentle folds of the hills. Softer, and grainier than Carboniferous limestone, it lies in an arc from the Isle of Portland in Dorset to the North Yorkshire coast. Steep west-facing escarpments, valleys and rolling countryside typify these landscapes, farmed for crops and sheep.

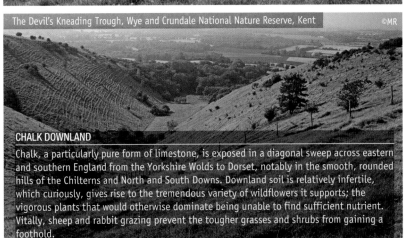
The Devil's Kneading Trough, Wye and Crundale National Nature Reserve, Kent
©MR

CHALK DOWNLAND

Chalk, a particularly pure form of limestone, is exposed in a diagonal sweep across eastern and southern England from the Yorkshire Wolds to Dorset, notably in the smooth, rounded hills of the Chilterns and North and South Downs. Downland soil is relatively infertile, which curiously, gives rise to the tremendous variety of wildflowers it supports; the vigorous plants that would otherwise dominate being unable to find sufficient nutrient. Vitally, sheep and rabbit grazing prevent the tougher grasses and shrubs from gaining a foothold.

On the farm

Arable fields near Kingston Lacy, Dorset ©DK

Much of the 'natural' landscape has evolved through generations of farming practice and, although apparently timeless, is continually changing. Stone Age farmers, clearing new land as soil became impoverished, unwittingly created the down, breck, heath and moor habitats we value today. Nomadism slowly gave way to settlement, creating early village and field systems as seen above Grassington (Yorkshire Dales), a pattern that continued until the Roman departure. The Saxons developed the rotational open field system, which at Laxton (Nottinghamshire) can still be visited, with three or four fields, woodland and grazing common surrounding each village. Many other ridge and furrow strips created by ox ploughing are marked on OS maps.

Two main factors wrought change during the medieval period – plague decimated the population, heralding the end of feudalism, and the spread of sheep farming saw vast tracts of arable land set to pasture. Deserted villages, often recognised by grassed mounds (Lower Harford, Cotswolds) or an isolated church (Wharram Percy, Yorkshire Wolds), can be found across the country. The Highland Clearances of the 18th and 19th centuries, also motivated by more profitable sheep farming, caused further massive depopulation and left many abandoned crofts (Lorgill, Skye).

The 18th century application of science to agriculture and husbandry wrought the next great landscape change, enclosure. Miles of stone wall, hedge or fence partitioned the open countryside into fields, while the mechanisation of farming accelerated the townward population drift. For the first time, the majority of the population was no longer employed on the land.

The drive for better yields and greater efficiency in food production from World War II onwards has dramatically altered farming practices and the landscape: habitat loss from the draining of wetlands and ploughing of heathland; loss of species diversity through intensive mono-crop agriculture; and abandonment of small, uneconomic upland farms. Increasingly though, farms are combining environmental awareness with profitability by promoting organic practices, leaving wide field margins and setting aside wildlife habitats.

CEREALS ▼

Crops serve many purposes and may be grown directly for human or animal consumption, for processing into industrial and food chain products, or for ploughing back as natural fertiliser. Cereals are grown countrywide, wheat tending to predominate towards the south and east with barley and oats farther north and west. Maize is less suited to the British climate and only in the south is it grown as sweet corn; elsewhere it is used as fodder.

Wheat

Barley

Oats

Maize

RAPESEED ▼

Swathes of brilliant yellow are a common sight on lowland farms in spring. Rapeseed's tiny black seeds are harvested to produce cooking oil and increasingly, biodiesel, while the residual meal is a nutritious livestock feed. Rapeseed is grown as a rotational 'break crop' to rejuvenate the soil. Bees are an important pollinator, although the honey quickly granulates and is usually blended for all-purpose use.

LAVENDER ▲

Less common are fields of purple or blue flowers. Lavender is grown for its oil, which is extracted by steam distillation and used in perfumery.

SUGAR BEET ▼

Sugar beet has been a major crop since the First World War and is mainly grown in eastern England. Harvested before the frost, it is processed in local factories to produce around 50% of Britain's sugar requirements. The leaves and residual pulp are fed to livestock.

FLAX ▼

Flax was once widely cultivated for fibre for cloth or rope manufacture but is now grown for seed used to produce linseed oil.

PASTURE ▶

Grass is Britain's main agricultural crop. Almost half the grazing is unimproved grassland, predominantly covering hillside, moor and heath, supporting low densities of animals (primarily sheep), and often rich in wildlife. Lees or water meadows are left to flood over winter, keeping off frost and encouraging an early crop of grass. These are disappearing but the Somerset Levels still provide classic wetland grazing. Chalk downs were some of the first areas to be cleared of woodland by prehistoric farmers, but the soils were soon impoverished and the land abandoned to grazing. Millennia of grazing has maintained the sward, creating Britain's most prolific wildflower habitat.

Virtually sterile as far as wildlife is concerned, but most productive for the farmer is rotational grass, which may be re-sown periodically where the field is used for other crops. Usually containing a single grass type and fertilised, it produces good grazing throughout the year and is mown in summer to produce silage. Whereas hay is cut and dried before storage, silage has high water content. Compressed into bales and covered with black plastic or stored in silage pits, it is left to ferment and fed to stock during the winter.

Silage making

Water meadows, Cambridgeshire

▼ BEEF CATTLE ▶

Selective breeding has produced specialised beef and dairy cattle. Traditional beef breeds include Hereford, Aberdeen Angus and English Longhorn, which more recently have been crossed with continental Charolais and Limousin to increase size and promote faster growth. Beef cattle reared in hill areas are often moved down to be fattened for market. The British beef herd is Europe's second largest after France and produces over two million head each year.

Aberdeen Angus

Hereford

English longhorn

DAIRY CATTLE

The most common dairy breed is the Holstein Friesian but others include Jersey, Guernsey and Ayrshire. Cows only produce milk after calving, but produce more offspring than necessary to maintain the herd, so the young bulls and surplus heifers are then reared for beef. Dairy cattle are found predominantly on lowland farms where grass growth is better. Cattle are overwintered indoors, being put out to pasture in spring as grass begins to grow. The small laithes or field-barns still seen in the Yorkshire Dales are the precursors of the large cattle sheds encountered on modern farms.

Holstein Friesian

Jersey

SHEEP ▼

There are more than 30 commercial sheep breeds in Britain. Typical hill breeds include Herdwick, kept for wool, and Swaledale, whose lambs generally go for meat. Although wandering free, sheep are 'hefted' to their own moor, lambs learning the geography from their mothers. Lowland sheep include the Suffolk, which produces fine meat, and the Romney Marsh known for its wool.

Swaledale

Suffolk

PIGS ▼

Pigs are seldom seen in the countryside, generally being reared in clinical indoor environments. But breeding sows and piglets might be seen as part of an arable farm, their arks or sties being warm, dry and providing protection from the sun. Still observed in the New Forest, pannage is the practice of turning out pigs into woodland to feed on fallen acorns in the autumn.

Large white

Gloucester old spot

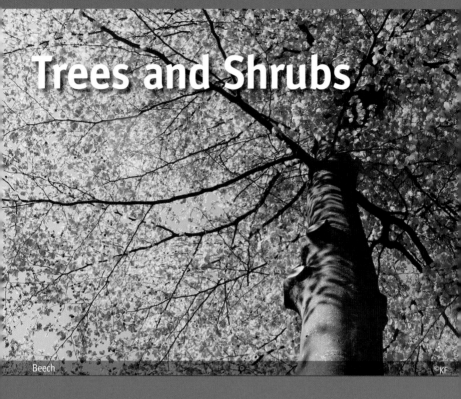

Trees and Shrubs

Beech ©KF

The improving climate following the last glacial period saw colonising species such as Scots pine and birch spread northwards, with alder, oak and others following. Species arriving in this way are regarded as native. This wildwood eventually covered most of the country. Deforestation began around 3500 BC, with Stone Age farmers clearing the land and, by the Norman Conquest, only 20% of forest cover survived. Woodland was intensively managed, but by the end of the First World War, less than 5% of Britain remained wooded. Since the establishment of the Forestry Commission in 1919, forest cover now approaches 12%.

Over 1,500 species of trees and shrubs grow in Britain, with around 80 being more commonly seen. Trees fall into two groups: **deciduous** or broad-leaved, which drop their leaves in winter, and **coniferous**, generally bearing needles and mostly evergreen (not shedding leaves for winter).

Beyond that, identification can be difficult and requires careful observation. The general shape of the tree can be important, but exposed positions and pruning can radically change its outline. Closer examination of leaves, flowers, fruit or nuts and seed bodies, depending upon the season, are all important aids to recognition. During winter the colour and texture of bark and arrangement of leaf buds will give clues to identification.

The ingenuity of nature has provided varied leaf forms and these give the biggest clues to tree identity. Beech leaves are oval, those of lime are heart-shaped, willows have slender ones, and oak leaves have lobed or wavy, indented edges. The horse chestnut and ash have compound leaves; the former having finger-like leaflets radiating from the end of a stem, while the ash can have between 6-12 paired leaflets along a single stem. Conifer needles can be long, like those of Scots pine, which sprout from a stem in pairs; spruce has short needles densely packed along a stem; and larch needles grow in small clusters.

BIRCH ▼

Both the silver birch and white or downy birch are native deciduous trees, early colonisers after the last glacial period. They are very hardy and can grow almost anywhere in Britain but are commonly found on dry and sandy soils. Easily becoming established on cleared ground, birches grow rapidly to between 50-70 feet (15-20m). With their light, fairly open foliage and distinctive pale, papery bark that peels in ribbon-like strips, they are rather attractive, elegant trees. The small leaves are heart-shaped with serrated edges and its catkins flower in April and May. The tree was revered and its twigs used for sweeping away evil, the same sentiment being behind its use as an instrument of punishment.

Silver birch catkins, spring

Silver birch seed heads, autumn

Silver birch woodland

OAK ▲

The oak has distinctively shaped, large-lobed leaves (adopted by the National Trust for its logo) and acorns (the National Trail symbol in England and Wales). However, look closely and you will see there are several types. The leaves of the traditional English, common or pendunculate oak sprout directly from the twig but the acorns are carried on stems (peduncles), while the durmast or sessile oak has the opposite arrangement. The acorns of the turkey oak sit in a 'mossy' cup.

Oak is slow-growing producing particularly good timber for construction, most notably once used for ship building. Trees develop vast root systems and not reaching maturity until at least 150 years of age, they can be long-lived – the Knightwood oak in the New Forest has a girth of 24 feet (7.4m) and is in excess of 400 years old. The branches and canopies of oaks are host to more than 400 species of insect.

POLLARDING, BEECH AND LIME

BEECH ▶

A magnificent native deciduous woodland tree, the beech is one of the country's tallest often attaining 100 feet (30m). It has a beautiful smooth grey bark. The foliage is densely packed and although bluebells may grow in early spring before the canopy is in full leaf, few other flowers can thrive in their heavy shade. Red helleborine is a rare plant of Cotswold and Chiltern beech woods. Bramblings are particularly fond of beech mast, sustaining them through the winter.

The stunningly coloured copper beech is not native and is planted largely for its decorative qualities.

Beech leaves and mast

Timber production in woodland and parkland estates could be maintained by **pollarding**, that is pruning the trees above the **graze-line** (far right), six to ten feet above ground level, where the new growth was out of reach of cattle and deer. Beech (right), oak and horse chestnut are among those that readily sprout new growth.

◀ LIME

The common lime is Britain's tallest deciduous tree and can reach 130 feet (40m) in height. It is frequently seen lining suburban avenues and in parks, large gardens and country estates – where much fashionable 17th-century ornamental planting took place. Limes have characteristic large burrs at the base of the tree from which spring an abundance of new growth. They have palm-sized, heart-shaped leaves and sweet-scented flowers (especially attractive to bees) that hang in small clusters below a long leaf-like bract. There are two other, less commonly seen lime species found in Britain: the large-leaved, which has larger leaves and can have a markedly wide spread and greater height, and the small-leaved, which is altogether smaller and tends to be found in old coppiced woodland. None of these trees are related to the citrus fruit of the same name.

ASH

The Norsemen regarded the ash as the tree of life and believed it had curative properties. The wood is hard and shock absorbent, and is used for manufacturing a whole range of articles from tool handles and hockey sticks to flooring and lobster pots. Easily identified in winter from its black buds, it has small, long oval leaves arranged in pairs along a stem that drop at the first hard frost, while the fruit hangs in dense clusters of winged seeds. It is one the latest native deciduous trees to come into leaf, usually in May and mature trees can average 50-100 feet (15-30m) in height.

WHITEBEAM ▼

A middle-sized tree of southern England growing to around 40 feet (12m), the whitebeam is more often seen in parks and gardens rather than in the wider countryside. Its fine-grained wood was once used for making cogs in gear wheels and in high-quality joinery. The underside of its leaves appear white, hence its name, being covered in felt-like hairs. The tree produces small red berries, which are eaten by birds.

HORNBEAM ▼

Related to the birch, the hornbeam also bears catkins and produces large, winged seeds. The leaves distinguish it from beech, which it may be mistaken for, by their corrugated leaf veins and unevenly serrated edges; the beech has smooth-edged leaves. It is a large tree and can grow to around 80 feet (25m) high, although was often managed by coppicing or pollarding. A tough, resilient wood, wheelwrights used it for crafting spokes and it was favoured for fabricating cogs in mill mechanisms.

Autumn leaves and fruit

CHESTNUTS AND LONDON PLANE

SWEET CHESTNUT ▶

Now widespread and naturalised, the sweet chestnut is thought to have been introduced by the Romans for its fruit, which is delicious roasted or boiled. It has long (8-inch, 20-cm), serrated leaves and the fruit is protected with a prickly shell. Mature trees can be impressively grand attaining a height of 100 feet (30m) and their trunk bark often displays a network of spiralling furrows.

LONDON PLANE ▼

Often planted as an avenue or street tree, the London plane has maple-like leathery leaves grown in pairs. Not indigenous, mature trees can reach 100 feet (30m) or so in height. It adapts well to city life, resisting pollution by periodically shedding its bark and the accumulated dirt. The fruit takes the form of small spiny baubles that remain affixed to the tree throughout the winter, only shedding them in spring.

HORSE CHESTNUT ▲

The spreading horse chestnut or conker tree is a completely different species and first made an appearance here in the late 16th century. It is a familiar sight in the countryside, particularly around villages and in parkland. With the red horse chestnut, it was often planted for its profusion of flowers or 'candles' that appear in May. In early spring the leaves emerge from large, sticky buds. The leaves are composed of five or seven leaflets radiating from the end of the stalk while the inedible conkers are contained in a hard spiny case.

ROWAN ▶

Few trees break the high moorland skyline but the rowan or mountain ash is one. It prefers light, acid soils and can grow at higher altitudes than most other trees. Rowans can grow to about 40 feet (12m) or so and each compound leaf usually consists of seven paired leaflets on one stem with a single leaflet at the end. In folklore the tree has many associations with magic and witchcraft, and was planted to ward off evil spirits, while the brilliant scarlet berries provide food for birds. The berries are also the prime ingredient in rowan jelly, which is served with game and red meat.

◀ SYCAMORE

Although now ubiquitous, the sycamore has only become widespread during the last 300 years. It is a very hardy member of the maple family and was often planted around farmsteads to afford protection and shade. It readily seeds and grows quickly, its dense foliage rapidly shading out the competition. Fully grown trees can exceed 100 feet (30m) in height though they support little insect life, on average only 19 species in comparison to over 400 benefiting from oak. Consequently it has become unwelcome and is being removed from many woods.

FIELD MAPLE ▶

The field maple is a small native deciduous tree of England and Wales, often found growing in hedges. It produces winged fruit similar to the sycamore and the leaves are small, dark and shiny with five characteristically maple-like lobes. The timber has a fine grain, ideal for carving, and it is used for making musical instruments, including the violin and harp.

COPPICING AND HEDGEROW TREES

HAZEL ▶

Hazel is a common small tree often seen in deciduous woodland growing as part of the understorey, and is also a good hedge plant. Once hazel had many uses and was often coppiced to ensure a regular supply of wood. Its bright yellow catkins, fondly called lamb's tails, are a familiar sight in February. The nuts develop in early autumn. Highly nutritious and a good source of vitamin E, they can be used in a variety of savoury and sweet recipes.

Enclosed woodland (to keep out grazing deer, cattle and pigs) was intensively managed by **coppicing**, cutting the tree back to the bole (base) to promote new growth. Occasional trees were left as standards for timber, but the regular crop of small wood was used for hurdle making and charcoal manufacture.

HOLLY ▼

Holly is Britain's commonest native evergreen and, associated now with Christmas decoration, it was the centrepiece of pre-Christian mid-winter customs. Its evergreen leaves and winter berries were seen as a symbol of eternity and it was regarded unlucky to

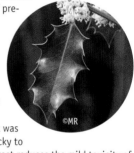

cut it down. Frost reduces the mild toxicity of the berries and they are winter food for many birds, particularly thrushes.

◀ CRAB APPLE

A small native fruit tree growing singly in woods and hedgerows, the crab apple is the origin of the huge variety of cultivated apples. Although its fruit is small and bitter, it makes excellent jelly and wine. The hard, fine-grained wood made it an excellent timber for carpenters and wood carvers.

WILD CHERRY ▶

Spring is on its way when the native wild cherry blooms, although its delicate flower clusters are often battered by winds, which always seem to hit just after they burst forth. Fruit arrives in mid summer and although smaller than the cultivated variety is often particularly sweet. The bird cherry, which grows in northern Britain, has black fruit that is rather bitter.

HAWTHORN ▶

Hawthorn is the commonest hedgerow bush, being a popular choice of hedging material when fields were first enclosed more than 300 years ago. Trees left as standards may reach 50 feet (15m). It is widely known as May, after the month in which it flowers, the blossom heralding the beginning of summer – hence the expression 'Never cast a clout, 'til May is out', meaning keep your winter clothes at hand until May is in flower. Hawthorn bears bright red berries in autumn.

ELDER ▲

Elder is a small deciduous tree and commonly seen among hedgerows. Although it gives off a rather unpleasant odour, both the flowers and densely clustered ripe berries are used to make very pleasant country wines. The flowers can produce a light white wine, reminiscent of a hock, which also works well if made into a sparkling wine. The berries can create a full-bodied red wine, but are also used for making jellies.

DOG ROSE ▶

Another attractive hedgerow bush is the dog rose, also popular in cottage gardens. Having a delicate scent, its petals were used to make rose water or dried for potpourri. The rose hips are rich in vitamin C and, during the Second World War the fruit was used to make rose hip syrup for young children.

BLACKTHORN ▼

Blackthorns are armed with tough spines and make good hedging shrubs, their white flowers being among the first in the spring hedgerow. Perhaps better known as sloe bushes, in the autumn they bear small, damson-like fruits that have little flesh and an astringent taste, but when soaked in gin with sugar make a fine liqueur – sloe gin.

HONEYSUCKLE ▼

The sweet scent and unusual flowers of honeysuckle are unmistakable. Sometimes called woodbine, it entwines within a hedge and was often grown around cottage doorways, the fragrance filling the house and supposedly preventing evil crossing the threshold. However, it was considered unlucky to bring it inside.

◀ ALDER

Alder is a native deciduous tree and anciently regarded as sacred. A member of the birch family, it grows in wet and marshy places and is characteristic of wet woodland. The alder is a noted coloniser species and is planted in land reclamation schemes. Trees usually attain heights of 65-80 feet (20-25m) and in early spring bear male and female catkins, the smaller fruiting female developing into a little cone. The timber is resistant to water and was often used for drinking troughs and bridge piles.

WEEPING WILLOW ▼

This is a non-native ornamental species popular in parks and gardens.

CRACK WILLOW ▲

The crack willow is so called for having brittle twigs and the fact that its trunk often cracks in old age. They are seen along ditches and at the margins of rivers, ponds and lakes where their roots help bind and stabilize the banks. The leaves are long (6 inches, 15cm) and slender, which distinguish it from the white willow whose leaves are shorter with felt-like silver hairs on their underside, hence the 'white' name. The white willow is a much larger tree and was often pollarded to provide withies for basket making.

GOAT WILLOW or SALLOW ▼

This is more popularly called pussy willow. It is Britain's commonest native willow and grows widely in almost any damp and wet place from ditches and waste ground to fenland. Pussy willow is most easily recognised in early spring from its yellow-tinged silvery catkin flowers, which appear before the leaves. These are oval, unlike leaves of other willows and the trees are small, rounded and bushy.

Ungrazed lowland wet meadows are likely to develop a covering of shrubs and trees, which can take hold to create a wet woodland habitat known as carr. Typically, alder and willows provide tree cover with a dense tangle of buckthorn, bramble and dog rose below.

SCOTS PINE ▶

Tolerant of poor ground and sandy soils, Scots pine was one of the first colonising trees to reach Britain and may live for 200 years. The Scots pine has long, paired bluish-green needles and pointed cones. Male and female flowers develop each year at the tip of the growing shoot, the wind releasing clouds of yellow pollen in spring. Cones develop over three years before releasing their seeds. The pinkish-brown bark is characteristic of younger trees. It is one of the strongest softwoods and the timber is used widely in the construction industry. The tree's tall, straight trunk was valued for ships' masts and planking while the resin was distilled to make turpentine. Much of the remaining ancient Caledonian pine forest in the Scottish Highlands, Britain's only native pine forest, is of Scots pine.

JUNIPER ▶

Juniper is quite rare and, contrastingly, is found on acid soils in the highlands, where it grows as a low and dense prickly bush, and on the chalk downlands of southern Britain, where it can also grow upright. Its seeds are contained in small green berries that ripen to a bluish purple and are used as flavouring, notably in gin. The wood produces a very pure charcoal.

◀ YEW

A yew in Fortingall's churchyard in Perthshire is regarded as Britain's oldest tree, having stood for more than 2,000 years. Often found in graveyards, the tree is associated with longevity and is a symbol of faith, its branches used to represent the Easter palm. Almost every part of the tree is poisonous particularly the seeds, although the surrounding red fleshy cups are attractive to birds, who then spread the seeds. Yew wood is strong and highly pliable and in medieval times was used for making longbows.

Juniper and silver birch woodland, Caingorms

NON-NATIVE CONIFERS

SPRUCE ▶

The needles of spruce are individually attached to the branch by a peg-like structure. The traditional Christmas tree, the Norway Spruce, has long, cylindrical cones and pointed, green needles. It has a tough, elastic timber, which is sold as white deal, although its acoustic properties lead it sometimes to be called violin wood. Now more commonly planted is the Sitka spruce, which does better in Britain's wet climate. Its sharp needles are flattened and have a blue tint while the cones, although similar to the Norway, have larger diamond-shaped scales.

DOUGLAS FIR ▲

Fir trees are characterised by flat needles. Brought back from the American west coast as an ornamental tree in 1827, the Douglas fir produces a quality wood used for veneer and plywood as well as timber in furniture and general construction. It has soft needles and a downward-pointing oval cone, the large scales each bearing a three-pointed bract. In Britain trees can attain 180 feet (55m) tall, but reach loftier heights in North America.

LARCH ▼

Introduced in the early 17th century both for its durable timber and decorative appeal, larch is the only European deciduous conifer. In autumn its needles turn a striking golden yellow and then fall to create a thick ground carpet. The needles are soft and bunched together like miniature shaving brushes, the small cones tending to stand upright.

◀ WESTERN HEMLOCK

Like firs, the hemlock family has flat needles. The western hemlock was introduced as an ornamental tree, but has some commercial use in packaging and paper-making. In its native North America the Indians used the inner bark for making bread. The branches are drooped rather than perky, its cones small and egg-shaped and the needles, when crushed release an aroma reminiscent of parsley.

Bee orchid ©MR

Flowers and fungi

Estimates for the number of wildflower species in Britain vary from 2,500 to 4,000, of which more than 200 are listed as rare or endangered and are thus protected. With so many, identification can be a headache, but a little practice and methodical observation will usually lead to the right answer. Leaves, flower-heads and seed pods appear at different times of the year and often several of these features need to be taken into account.

Understanding the various parts of the flower is a good starting point. Most flowers have petals, which attract pollinators and surround the reproductive parts of the plant; the stamens, which carry the pollen and the stigma, the female part, which receives the pollen and goes on to produce the seed. Beneath the petals are sepals, petal-like and often green, which protected the developing flower bud. Bracts are modified leaves, which may sometimes look like petals. The stem supporting the flower may bear leaves, but they might alternatively sprout directly from the base. However, flowers are infinitely variable and the different parts may not always be present or immediately recognisable.

Look at the plant closely, noting flower structure, colour, number of petals, shape and distribution of leaves, whether hairy or succulent, and the habitat in which it is growing. A photograph is a good aide memoir; picking is not for they quickly wither and become unrecognisable. It is illegal to uproot any flower, as is picking any of the rare or vulnerable species.

There are more than 300 species of sedges, rushes, grasses and ferns in Britain. Although often seemingly insignificant, they display great variety and most bear fascinating tiny flowers and seed pods.

Stranger still are the 500 or more species of fungi. They colonise many habitats, even bleak windswept moors, but we most frequently associate them with woodland.

COTTON GRASS ▲

Often seen in carpeting swathes, cotton grass is unmistakable in early summer – a plant of acid bogs and fens. The white, fluffy seed-heads were once used for candlewicks, but the wary walker will steer clear, for they often mark waterlogged ground.

BITING STONECROP ▲

Biting stonecrop is a perennial succulent with yellow star-shaped flowers from May to July, widespread in a range of rough, well-drained habitats from coasts to mountainsides; and often seen on walls or paving forming dense mats.

SPHAGNUM ▼

Sphagnum mosses are small plants that grow together in carpets on wet ground on moors and heaths and can form large sponge-like hummocks. They derive nutrients directly from rainwater and, amazingly, can retain large amounts of it long after the surrounding ground has dried. Absorbent and slightly antiseptic it served as wound dressings during two World Wars.

MOUNTAIN AVENS ▼

The mountain avens is confined to rocky, upland terrain in Snowdonia, northern England and northern Scotland. It flowers in June and July and has leaves not unlike a miniature oak.

COMMON ROCK-ROSE ▲

A widespread perennial flowering from June to September, the common rock-rose favours short turf in open scrub and grasslands.

MOUNTAIN PANSY ▼

The pansy from the French *pensée,* is a close relation to the violet and is a symbol of love or remembrance. The mountain pansy flowers from June to August growing on short-cropped turf of the uplands of Wales, northern England and Scotland.

BELL HEATHER ▶

Bell heather is an evergreen shrub whose purple flowers carpet heaths and moors in late summer. Its small leaves are arranged in whorls around the stem. Left unmanaged, heather becomes woody, but rotational burning encourages new growth for sheep and grouse.

LING ▼

Bell heather and ling both favour drier ground and grow together, but ling has a much smaller, paler flower. Also an evergreen, its leaves are small and oppositely arranged on woody stems.

BUTTERWORT ▼

An insectivorous plant, each leaf in the butterwort's rosette of leaves, has an inward curving edge and sticky glands on its upper surface which attract insects, each plant consuming an estimated 5,000 per year. A single flower spike is produced in summer.

BROOM ▲

Displayed in May and June, broom has similar flowers to gorse but, distinguishingly, it lacks the sharp spines. It was used to make brooms, hence its name, and is an ancestor of today's garden varieties although its flowers are unscented.

BOG ASPHODEL ▲

Giving clumped splashes of vivid yellow, bog asphodel flowers from July to September. It is known in Lancashire as maiden hair since young lassies used it to dye their tresses.

GORSE ▶

Gorse, sometimes called furze, is a prickly evergreen shrub that produces sweet-scented yellow flowers throughout the year but with peak flowering periods in early spring and late summer. It burns well and, in times past, was often cut for fuel, while young shoots were harvested for livestock fodder in harsh winters.

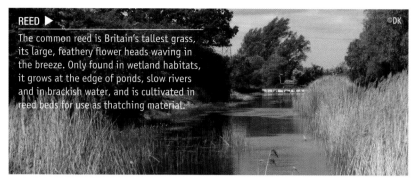

REED ▶

©DK

The common reed is Britain's tallest grass, its large, feathery flower heads waving in the breeze. Only found in wetland habitats, it grows at the edge of ponds, slow rivers and in brackish water, and is cultivated in reed beds for use as thatching material.

REEDMACE ▼

Reedmace has impressive club-like seed heads. You may know it as the bulrush, but that is a type of sedge having tall, needle-like leaves and tassels of small brown flowers in late summer. It is believed the confusion derives from a picture by the Victorian artist Alma-Tadema, who depicted Moses amongst the more impressive reedmace.

TEASEL ▲

Liking damp ground around water margins, the teasel was once grown commercially and used as a comb for raising the nap on woollen cloth. They can grow to 6 feet (1.8m) tall and attract goldfinches in the autumn.

RAGGED ROBIN ▼

Becoming less common is the delicate ragged robin, which likes damp meadows and woodland fringes and according to folklore, if picked, was believed to induce a thunderstorm.

©MR

WATER AVENS ▼

Seen flowering from May to September in shady damp places, the beautiful water avens is widespread but commoner in northern England, Wales and Scotland. Its powdered root was once mixed with brandy to alleviate malaria.

©DK

SEDGE

The sedge family display great variety and most bear fascinating small flower spikelets and seed pods. Looking rather like tall grasses, sedges grow in marshy and wetland areas and include species such as cotton grass and spike rush, both common across upland moors. Whereas grass stems have a circular cross-section, those of sedge are usually triangular. Most grow in tight clumps or spreading rhizomes.

MARSH MARIGOLD ▶

Similar in appearance to buttercups, the marsh marigold or king cup has much larger flowers and grows in wet meadows, riverbanks, ponds and marshes, liking shady and dappled sunlight. It flowers from March through to October.

YELLOW FLAG ▲

Flowering from May to July, the tall yellow flag particularly likes river banks and wet ditches, and is found around pond edges. It was adopted by Louis VII as the *fleur-de-lys*.

COMFREY ▼

Comfrey favours damp wetland margins and is sometimes called knit-bone; the leaves and roots once used to treat skin complaints as well as fractured bones. The flowers appear in May and June ranging from creamy-white to purplish.

WHITE WATER-LILY ▶

Lakes at lower elevations can support a wealth of plants, particularly in their shallow and marshy perimeters. In summer, lily pads can almost cover the ponds at Bosherston in Pembrokeshire. The white water-lily is found almost exclusively in still water whereas the yellow water-lily, which has the largest leaves of Britain's water plants, favours a gentle river.

LADY'S SMOCK ▼

Lady's smock is alternatively known as cuckoo flower because it blooms in April and May when cuckoos are first heard.

PURPLE LOOSESTRIFE ▼

A common and widespread perennial, purple loosestrife colonises riverbanks and wet ditches and flowers in June through to August.

EARLY PURPLE ORCHID ▼

An indicator of ancient deciduous woodland, the early purple orchid flower spikes appear in

April and May. Its leaves are spotted. The plant's twin tubers were likened to testicles and, mixed with milk, were drunk as an aphrodisiac.

MAIDENHAIR SPLEENWORT ▼

The damp dark conditions of woodland favour ferns – ancient, non-flowering plants that reproduce using spores produced on the underside of long,

fronded leaves – like the delicate-looking maidenhair spleenwort, which grows on banks and old walls.

WOOD ANEMONE ▼

Wood anemone, also known as windflower, whose white flowers can have a lilac or pink blush, carpets deciduous woodland floors in April.

LESSER CELANDINE ▲

The lesser celandine is an early spring flower of hedgerows and woodlands, but prefers damp ground and likes the sun, closing its yellow flower on dull days. Distinguished by heart-shaped fleshy leaves, it was a favourite of Wordsworth, who composed a poem about it. Less romantically, it was held to be a cure for piles, hence its other name – pilewort.

WOOD-SORREL ▲

Widespread on shaded floors of damp deciduous woodland, wood-sorrel has delicate clover-like leaves grouped in threes. These only fully open in shade; if met directly with the sun's rays they fold into inverted cone-shapes held against the stem. Candle of the woods is one of its many common names.

HART'S TONGUE FERN ▼

The descriptively-named hart's-tongue fern, which has long unlobed leaves, can typically be seen on the shaded banks of old sunken lanes and tracks through mature woodland.

Micheldever Wood, Hampshire

◀ **BLUEBELL**

Bluebell woodland is a wonderful spectacle in May. The Tudors used crushed bulbs as a starch and made glue that served both bookbinders and fletchers – for sticking flights on to arrows.

RHODODENDRON ▼

Rhododendron was introduced in the late 18th century and planted extensively by the Victorians for its colourful flowers and as game cover on country estates. However, its rampant growth and vigorous propagation out-competes other plants and, unchecked, it can invade large areas of woodland and heath, destroying valuable wildlife habitats.

FOXGLOVE ▼

The foxglove is a tall plant exploiting woodland clearings, its name perhaps deriving from Anglo-Saxon and meaning *fairy bells* by which it is occasionally known. A biennial, it flowers only during its second year, the bells usually purple but occasionally white. Although poisonous, its leaves have a medical application in controlling heart rate, which was discovered in 1785.

ROSEBAY WILLOWHERB ▶

Found along verges, forest rides and in areas of felled woodland, rosebay willowherb is an early coloniser of cleared ground and wasteland. Named after its narrow willow-like leaves, it is sometimes known as fireweed for its propensity to spring up after fire, and it quickly covered bombsites during the Second World War.

BRACKEN ▶

Bracken favours open, well-drained ground and can be identified by fronded leaves branching from a stem that can grow to over 6 feet (1.8m). Also found on moors and heaths, it is poisonous to horses and cattle.

RAMSONS ▼

Ramsons thrive in damp conditions on riverbanks, shaded woodland and hedgerow verges. Also known as wild garlic, its heavy scent betrays its presence before it is seen. Leaves and bulbs were used by herbalists in treating asthma and lung conditions, while the milk of cows grazing upon them produced a subtly garlic-flavoured butter.

The most abundant wildflower grasslands are hay meadows and downs; old grazing that has been traditionally managed over the centuries. Livestock may be briefly turned out on meadows in early spring, but the fields are then left for the grass to grow to maturity in June. This enables the plants shown here to flower and set seed before the hay is cut. Returning livestock then naturally manure the field before winter.

MEADOW BUTTERCUP ▼

Meadow buttercup carpets hay meadows and are loved by children to determine who likes butter. Flowering from early spring to late summer, they are poisonous and avoided by cattle.

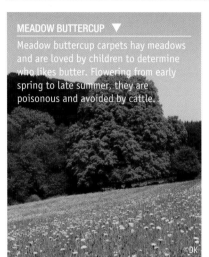

COWSLIP ▼

Found on unimproved grassland across England and Wales, cowslips like the close-cropped turf produced by grazing sheep and rabbits, flowering in April and May.

RED CLOVER ▷

Clover enriches the soil with nitrogen and makes excellent fodder for livestock. The leaves have variegated white markings and, it is considered lucky to find a four-leaved clover, as they more usually grow in threes.

GREATER KNAPWEED ▼

Greater knapweed is found extensively on calcareous soils in England and Wales. It is a late summer flower and its purple compound flower heads are larger than those of common knapweed.

DEVIL'S BIT SCABIOUS ▼

One of three native scabious species, the devil's bit scabious flowers from June until September across the country, in grassland habitats and verges.

◁ HORSESHOE VETCH

Large areas of unimproved grassland support a wide assortment of flowers. Horseshoe vetch is common, its pea-shaped flower adapted to deliver pollen to bees alighting on the lower petal.

PYRAMIDAL ORCHID ▶

The pyramidal orchid produces a tight cluster of tiny flowers in a dense spike on a single stem. It favours the chalk downland of southern England.

◀ RIBWORT PLANTAIN

Abundant and widespread, they have tall stems and brown cylindrical heads covered with small creamy-white flowers and ribbed leaves. They are also called rat-tails, among many other local names.

YELLOW RATTLE ▼

Also known as hay rattle, this common grassland annual is in flower from May to July. It develops a capsule containing large seeds which, when shaken, make a rattling sound.

FIELD POPPY ▶

Field poppies are coming back to cornfields.
Their seeds can remain dormant for decades, but turn the soil and they sprout; the reason that they grew in profusion on the disturbed ground of the Flanders' battlefields. They became a symbol of remembrance of all those who lost their lives and the first British Legion Poppy Day was held in 1921.

BUGLE ▼

Widespread in woodlands and meadows, bugle is scentless and attracts bees by its vivid blue colour, but more commonly propagates from rooting stems. It flowers during May, June and July.

VIPER'S BUGLOSS ▲

Viper's bugloss is in bloom from May to September and favours chalky and sandy soils. Its upright flower spike has a hairy stem. Although mildly toxic, the 17th-century herbalist Nicholas Culpeper recommended it to improve the milk flow of nursing mothers and alleviate lumbago.

STINGING NETTLE ▲

Although much maligned, the common nettle was once considered rather useful. The versatile leaves of young plants can be served as a vegetable or made into soup, flavour cheese or make a refreshing beer. During the Second World War the leaves were used to dye camouflage nets. The Romans applied nettles to their joints to relieve rheumatism. It is the caterpillar foodplant for several of our butterflies (see pages 77-78) and is the focus of the annual nettle-eating contest at Marshwood in Dorset.

DEAD-NETTLE ▶

The red and white dead-nettles are a good source of nectar for bees in early spring. They continue flowering into autumn and although they appear similar to the common nettle, as their names suggest, they do not sting.

YELLOW ARCHANGEL ▼

The leaves of yellow archangel also give it a nettle-like appearance. The yellow flowers are seen on banks and hedgerows in spring. It is more common and widespread in southern Britain.

BROAD-LEAVED DOCK ▲

Broad-leaved dock is often found growing close to common nettles and a bruised leaf rubbed on the skin has provided relief from the nettle's sting for generations, although in fact this is probably a placebo effect. Like the many other members of the dock and sorrel family, they have a long tap root and green, inconspicuous flowers clustering upon long stems.

COMMON BURDOCK ▼

The clustered and compound flower heads look similar to thistles and have hooked barbs surrounding them, which can become caught on the coats of animals (and passing walkers) and are thus scattered. The stalks were once boiled to make an aphrodisiac.

PRIMROSE ▷

Abundant in early spring, the primrose is sacred to Freyja, the Norse god of love, the five petals of each flower symbolise life – in birth, initiation, consummation, repose and death. Finding a rare six-petal flower brought happiness in love and marriage. The plant would supposedly point the way to the land of the fairies and, perhaps for this reason, Victorians planted it upon children's graves.

SWEET VIOLET ▽

Violets are often found in clusters on verge banks in early spring. Oil of sweet violet is used both as a fragrance in toiletries and flavouring in confectionery and was once strewn on floors to freshen the room. The scent contains a chemical that dulls the sense of smell and while the violet's scent is soon lost, so too are undesirable odours. Although similar looking, the dog violet has no scent.

CHICORY ▽

The sky-blue flowered chicory is a member of the daisy family. It is tall (more than 3 feet, 1m) and flowers July to October. Its dried and ground roots are used to flavour coffee, famously Camp Coffee, manufactured in Scotland since 1885. The plant's leaves can be used as both a salad and vegetable.

GERMANDER SPEEDWELL ▽

Flowering in spring and summer, this is probably the commonest of more than a dozen varieties of speedwell found in Britain. The name is believed to derive from 'farewell' or 'speed you well' as the petals drop soon after picking and so the flowers are soon gone.

FORGET-ME-NOT ▲

The last words of a German knight, swept away in sudden flood while picking pretty, blue flowers for his sweetheart from the riverbank, are believed to give the forget-me-not its name. Like speedwell, it has small blue flowers but the leaves are larger and more elongated.

RED CAMPION ▶

Widespread along lane verges and hedgerows, the pink flowers appear in May and June. Named after Silenus, the drunken Greek god of the woodland, red campion (silene dioica) has many associations with fairies, goblins and devils. Attracting bees, it was said to guard the honey store of the fairies while more sinisterly, if picked, could bring about the death of one's parents.

COW PARSLEY ▲

Found in overgrown verges and meadows, its white flowers appear in spring and early summer. Cow parsley can grow to around 3 feet (1m) and each stem, which is unspotted, can carry six to ten branches, known as rays, with each ray branching again to carry the flowers.

ALEXANDERS ▼

Having greenish-yellow flowers and also arranged in a compound umbrel, Alexanders is named after the great Macedonian ruler and tasting of celery, was common in medieval monastic gardens.

HOGWEED ▼

There are many different types of parsley, all having clustered flowers radiating umbrella-like from stem branches. Hogweed has distinctive broad rhubarb-like leaves covered on both sides with bristly hairs. It has an erect, ridged stem reaching up to 6½ feet (2m) in height. Unmistakable is the giant hogweed, which grows to more than 10 feet (3m) and has sap that blisters the skin.

GREAT MULLEIN ▶

Clustered with yellow flowers, the conspicuous spikes of great mullein or Aaron's rod can grow to 5 feet (1.5m). It likes a sunny aspect on well-drained rough ground. Also called the candlewick plant, the hairy leaf down (giving the leaves a whitish appearance) readily burns and was used for wicks and in tinder boxes. Another old name is bullock's lungwort, the plant being fed to cattle to cure a cough.

OX-EYE DAISY

The name daisy supposedly derives from 'day's eye', since the flower closes at nightfall. The ox-eye is a tall plant with big flower heads. The nickname 'Daisy' for 'Margaret' derives from the plant's French name 'Marguerite'. Infusions of the flowers were given to relieve whooping cough and asthma and a lotion alleviated bruises and chapped hands.

WILD ARUM ▼

One of the most exotic-looking plants is wild arum, which has a profusion of local names including lords and ladies and cuckoo pint, the unusual shape of the hooded flower invoking many sexual overtones. The plant is pollinated by flies, which are attracted by the smell of decay it emits. During autumn, red berries form which, like the rest of the plant, are poisonous. The tuber was used by the Tudors to starch fashionable ruffs.

DANDELION ▼

The dandelion is also a member of the daisy family, the flower head composed of numerous florets, each producing a tufted seed that disperses with the wind. Children blew on them to tell time, each puff being an hour, while maidens would try to blow them all off in one go to determine the depth of their beau's love.

TANSY ▼

Tansy is a tall perennial and its compound yellow flowers crowd in flat-topped clusters. They appear from July to September. The leaves have a spicy scent and bitter taste that was once used as a flavouring.

RAGWORT ▲

The golden yellow florets form in dense clusters to give a large flower head atop a straight stem that can grow to 4 feet (1.25m). It is poisonous to horses and cattle, but the larval foodplant of the cinnabar moth whose bright yellow-orange and black banded caterpillars can strip a plant bare.

SCARLET PIMPERNEL ▶

These little red flowers that give the plant its name are found around the margins of cultivated fields, verges and on rough ground. It is considered an agricultural weed. The flowers close when there is an increase in humidity, giving rise to its other common name – poor-man's weather glass.

HERB ROBERT ▼

Herb Robert is an annual and member of the geranium family. Its small pink flowers can be seen throughout the summer in deciduous woodland, on all types of waste ground and among coastal rocks and on shingle.

WILD STRAWBERRY ▼

Flowering throughout the summer in hedgerows and deciduous woodland fringes, the wild strawberry plant is smaller than the cultivated species and its unmistakable fruit is smaller and produced in fewer numbers. The berries are very popular with birds.

BINDWEED ▼

Bindweed is a prolific climber found along hedges, walls and ditches. It has big, white funnel-shaped flowers, which appear from July to September, and twisting around neighbouring vegetation it can gain great height – up to 10 feet (3m). Its relation, lesser bindweed, is a low climber and spreads across the ground around field edges, and has smaller white flowers with a pale pink blush.

TRAVELLER'S JOY ▼

In autumn and winter this wild clematis displays the grey tufted balls of long, silky hairs, which give rise to its other common name – old man's beard. The plant entwines amongst hedge branches and in spring produces clusters of white flowers. In France it is known as the beggar's herb; the irritant sap being used to redden and inflame the skin to attract more sympathy.

MARRAM GRASS ▶

Dune plants are highly specialised and vital for stabilisation, for without their binding roots the sand would just as easily disperse. Marram grass has leaves evolved to reduce moisture loss and deep roots to tap groundwater.

◀ SEA CAMPION

The white summer flowers of sea campion may be seen all round Britain's coast, particularly liking the short turf of cliff tops alongside other plants such as wild thyme, kidney vetch (locally known as buttery-fingers or lady's fingers from its yellow finger-like bracts) and Hottentot fig.

THRIFT ▶

Also known as sea pink, the flowers may be seen from March through to October right around the British coast. On salt marshes grazed by sheep, carpets of thrift can become turf-like. Thrift is also found on inland cliffs, walls and rocky upland areas.

◀ COMMON SCURVY-GRASS

Scurvy-grass, a member of the cabbage family, is rich in vitamin C and was eaten by sailors to prevent scurvy. It has a long flowering season from spring through to autumn.

SEA KALE ▼

Another member of the cabbage family, sea kale is only found on seashore and sea cliff habitats, and has small white summer flowers.

YELLOW HORNED POPPY ▼

The yellow horned poppy manages to survive on the apparently inhospitable bare shingle around the seashore of England, Wales and southern Scotland. Its flowering season is from June to October.

FUNGI

More closely related to animals than plants, fungi form a completely separate kingdom that ranges from yeasts and moulds to toadstools. Some like the ink cap absorb nutrition from decaying plant matter, while others such as bracket fungi parasitise living plants.

Bracket fungus

STINKHORN ▲

The foul-smelling stinkhorn is unmistakable too; a thick, white stalk with a black tapering honeycombed cap that secretes a sticky substance attractive to insects, which then disperse the spores. Despite its unattractive appearance, it is not poisonous.

◄ FLY AGARIC

Easily recognised, the fly agaric grows amongst birch and pine trees. Red with white spots, it is the toadstool of children's storybooks, but is a poisonous hallucinogen and was once crushed in milk to kill flies.

Autumn is the best time to see fungi. The more obvious types like the parasol mushroom are commonly found in meadows and woodland edges. Some make good eating and, like the prized truffle, can be a rare delicacy. Others contain deadly poisons, occasionally nullified by cooking, but a few, more insidious, produce liver failure only after several days. The only sound advice is, **unless absolutely sure, leave it alone.**

Parasol mushroom

◄ PUFF BALL

Puff balls have the largest fruiting body of native fungi and can grow to football-size. When mature, it will burst at the slightest touch, releasing trillions of powdery spores.

ORANGE PEEL ▶

Orange peel's irregular cup-shaped fruiting bodies are found on bare ground and, as the name suggests, resemble strewn orange peel.

Mammals

Hazel dormouse ©MR

There are over 60 wild mammal species breeding in Britain. The more common animals, such as grey squirrels, rabbits and foxes might be spotted on any countryside walk and, dependent upon season, seals can be a common sight along parts of the coast. More secretive are rats, wood mice, field voles and badgers, but they are equally prevalent and usually not far away.

Urbanisation and intensive farming have diminished many habitat opportunities, but some animals, particularly rats and foxes have actively exploited Man's environment and do quite well, even in cities. However, other species, such as red squirrel, dormouse and pine marten are declining in numbers and without active intervention to conserve habitats (or eliminate the competition), will become increasingly rare. Indeed some mammals have gone altogether; brown bears were hunted to extinction during Roman times and beavers, wild boars and wolves disappeared during the medieval period. In fact, the first beavers to live in Scotland for 400 years were reintroduced in 2009 by the Scottish Wildlife Trust.

Other animals that we regard as 'native' have in fact been introduced. The Normans brought over rabbits and 'farmed' them in pillow mounds to provide a ready source of meat and fur, while the grey squirrel arrived from North America as a novelty to adorn Victorian parks and woodlands. Along with mink, imported during the 1960s to stock fur farms, they have adapted so well to the British countryside that they are regarded a pest in many areas. Some of our larger mammals such as fallow, Sika and muntjac deer are also imports. More recent introductions include a small herd of reindeer roaming the Cairngorm and breeding populations of wild boar becoming re-established in Dorset, the Forest of Dean, East Sussex and Devon. There is even controversial talk of reintroducing wolves into the Scottish Highlands to help control the red deer population.

DEER AND FERAL GOAT

RED DEER ▶

This native deer is Britain's largest land mammal, found in south-west England, the New Forest, East Anglia and, principally, in the islands and highlands of Scotland, roaming open mountainside and forest and descending to lower ground in winter. During the autumn rut, impressively antlered stags will compete for the hinds, roaring, posturing and fighting rival males to assert dominance of the herd.

FALLOW DEER ▼

Fallow deer, commonly sporting a mottled fawn coat, are well established in much of England, Wales and southern Scotland. They are sometimes farmed for their venison and many country estates have grazing herds. The buck has palmate antlers – the angle between the points is partly filled to form a broad surface.

SIKA DEER ▲

Sika deer are related to red deer and can have similar antlers, but are much smaller with a dappled summer coat resembling the fallow deer. Accidentally or deliberately released from parks, they have become established in the New Forest, the Forest of Bowland, southern Cumbria and Scotland.

FERAL GOAT ▼

There are several herds of feral goat roaming remote hillsides of Wales and Scotland. Groups can also be found in the Cheviot Hills and around Lynton Gorge in Devon. Horned, hairy and shy, they are descendants of goats introduced by Neolithic farmers and are very nimble climbers.

ROE DEER ▼

Also native, but reintroduced following near extinction during the 19th century, is the smaller roe deer, recognised by its white rump. The stag's antlers rarely exceed three points and like all deer, shed them after the rut. They are relatively common in woodlands and forests throughout the country and are best spotted when grazing during late evening or early morning.

PONIES ▶

Herds of semi-wild ponies exist on Dartmoor, Exmoor, in the New Forest, the Welsh Hills, the Cumbrian Howgills and on some Scottish islands. In the past, these small, sturdy beasts were worked as pit ponies, while Princetown's prison guards rode Dartmoor ponies when escorting prisoners. Most herds are lightly managed and provided with extra food during winter.

Exmoor pony

◀ FOX

Foxes are a common sight across the countryside, their long, bushy tail and ruddy fur immediately recognisable. They will eat just about anything from berries and insects to small mammals and birds and are equally adept at scavenging suburban dustbins as seeking carrion on open moors.

BROWN HARE ▼

Larger than rabbits and with long ears, hares are much less common, and rather than burrows, make nests in long grass called forms or scrapes. Fast running and with phenomenal acceleration, they sit tight to the ground when danger nears leaving them vulnerable during crop spraying and harvest. Most likely seen in open fields in spring, their chasing and boxing antics give rise to the expression 'as mad as a March hare'. The mountain hare is a distinct species indigenous in Scotland and re-intorduced in the Peak District.

RABBIT ▼

Britain's rabbit population increased to pest proportions during the 19th century, causing considerable crop damage. But the population decimation following the 1950s myxomatosis outbreak brought problems too, as ungrazed heaths, dunes and chalk grassland reverted to scrub destroying habitats for other wildlife.

RED SQUIRREL ▼

The native red squirrel is increasingly a rare sight in Britain, becoming confined to pine woods where they feed off small-seeded cones. The best places to see reds are Scotland and northern England and the colonies at Formby, on Anglesey and the Isle of Wight.

GREY SQUIRREL

Grey squirrels thrive on a wide range of nuts and seeds and, in mixed woodland, steadily out-compete red squirrels for available food. Greys also carry a disease to which they are immune but which is often fatal to reds.

HEDGEHOG ▼

Living in hedge banks, woodlands and of course around gardens, hedgehogs are readily recognisable by their spines. They live off worms, slugs and crawling insects, fattening themselves in the autumn for winter hibernation in a small nest of leaves tucked under a bush or fallen bough.

WEASEL ▼

At around 10 inches (25cm) long, nose to tail tip, the weasel is Britain's smallest native carnivore. Having a long, slender body with a brownish upper coat and pale belly, they hunt mice, voles and occasionally rats, and are quite common where there is abundant prey.

WATER VOLE ▼

The water vole is the size of a rat, but has a more rounded face and furry tail. They may be seen either swimming or scurrying along the leafy banks of slow-moving rivers, canals and ditches into which they burrow. They eat plants and grasses growing on or near the water.

STOAT ▲

Larger than a weasel, a stoat has a characteristic dark tip to its tail. Its fur may turn white in winter, when it becomes known as ermine. They also feed on rodents but prefer bigger prey such as rabbits. In fact, the stoat nearly died out when the rabbit population succumbed to myxomatosis.

VOLES ▶

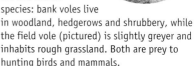

Voles are smaller and stouter than mice and have a short tail. Found countrywide, there are two similar species: bank voles live in woodland, hedgerows and shrubbery, while the field vole (pictured) is slightly greyer and inhabits rough grassland. Both are prey to hunting birds and mammals.

OTTER ▲

With a long, sleek, brown-furred body, powerful tail and webbed feet, the otter is perfectly adapted for its aquatic lifestyle. Found in best numbers along the north and west coasts of Scotland, elsewhere they range alongside rivers or lakes in Devon, Cornwall, the Lake District and Wales. Otters became rare due to loss of habitat and pesticide pollution, but recent conservation efforts have shown a small but promising increase in suitable habitat across the country.

COMMON SEAL

Adults reach 5½ feet (1.7m) in length. Their shorter muzzles with v-shaped nostrils and more rounded face distinguish them from grey seals, which have longer muzzles and parallel nostrils. They haul themselves on shore to bask, moult and mate. Females (cows) give birth to a single pup in June or July. The young are well developed at birth and can swim within hours, enabling common seals to breed in the relative safety of sand banks exposed by the ebb tide.

GREY SEAL ▼

Confusingly, the grey seal is more numerous than the common seal and about half the world's population gathers around Britain's coastline. They are variable in colour, despite their name, from creamy white through brown to dark grey, and usually with darker blotches. Males (bulls) can attain 7½ feet (2.3m) in length. A good time to see them is in autumn, when females beach in inaccessible coves to pup. The young remain ashore for three weeks, suckled on rich milk that enables them to gain on average over four pounds (2kg) a day.

One of the best places to observe marine mammals is in the waters around the Orkney Islands. There are large resident populations of common and grey seals and, offshore, sightings of minke and humpback whales are not unusual. Chanonry Point on the Moray Firth is also excellent for seal watching. Both seal species breed on the Norfolk coast and colonies of greys can be found on the Farne Islands and the Pembrokeshire and Cornish coasts.

BOTTLENOSE DOLPHIN ▼

There are five species of dolphin, the most frequently seen being the bottlenose dolphin, which is known to breed in Cardigan Bay and the Moray Firth. They have a blue-grey back, a pale underside and a dark dorsal fin that has a swept-back leading edge. Always active they can be seen typically leaping from the water or riding a bow wave.

Birds

Robin ©MR

With some 500 species visiting or resident in Britain, birds are everywhere, but identifying them is not always easy, even for the experts. However, a systematic approach will guide you in the right direction. Take note of the size; roughly comparing it with readily recognisable species such as sparrow, blackbird, duck or goose. The shape is also relevant; some birds such as the swallow have sleek bodies, while others are quite stocky like the partridge. Look at the beak too; some are long or delicate for probing such as curlew and oystercatcher, others short, perhaps hooked for tearing meat like the buzzard's or robust for cracking seeds like the hawfinch. The legs may be long for wading or short for perching and the feet webbed, clawed or having talons. Colour and markings are important, although not always straightforward. Males, females and juveniles will often be quite different and some birds alter their plumage during the breeding season or in winter. The plumage of the ptarmigan, living in the harsh mountains of the Scottish Highlands, changes colour with the seasons from grey-brown to white to camouflage it against bare rock in summer and snow fields in winter. The context in which the bird is seen may also be helpful; woods, open countryside, moors, water or coast generally attract their own particular species, but remember that some birds are adaptable to different environments. Finally, listen for the song or call. You may hear an owl, cuckoo or woodpecker without a chance of seeing it while songbirds are establishing territories and seeking the attention of a mate.

ROBIN ▲

Although noted for tameness from its habit of pinching worms from the feet of a digging gardener, in its more natural woodland setting, the robin is a rather wary bird. It is also aggressively territorial, fiercely chasing off interlopers. Nevertheless, its endearing qualities have led to it being unofficially adopted as Britain's national bird.

BLUE TIT ▶

Originally a woodland bird, the blue tit is common in parks, gardens and hedgerows. It is a popular visitor to bird feeders where its agile and acrobatic feeding habits can best be observed. They are widespread across Britain eating small insects and caterpillars as well as seeds and nuts.

◀ GREAT TIT

This is the largest British tit, about the same size as a house sparrow. In spring its loud 'tea-cher, tea-cher, tea-cher' call is distinctive. They are found countrywide in woodlands, parks and gardens. A breeding pair may hatch 8 to 12 young, which are fed largely on caterpillars, consuming in total an estimated 7,500 in the three weeks prior to fledging.

CRESTED TIT ▶

Identified by its black and white crest, in Britain it is confined to the pine woodland and plantations of the Highlands of Scotland. It feeds mainly on insects picked from the trunk and branches of pines, sometimes taking the seeds from pine cones and juniper berries.

COAL TIT ▶

Smaller than the blue tit and more muted in colour than the great tit, it is also shyer and although it will visit feeders in parks and gardens, chiefly feeds on insects in coniferous trees and woodland. It has a distinguishable white patch on the back of its neck.

LONG-TAILED TIT ▲

These pretty tits have pink, white and black plumage with a characteristic black and white tail which, at 3 inches (7.5cm), is longer than its body. They have an undulating flight and are usually seen in small flocks in woods, hedgerows and scrubland bushes searching noisily for insects.

BEARDED TIT ▶

The 'beard' is in fact a black moustache-like stripe on the male. Associated only with reed beds, bearded tits are wetland birds of eastern and southern England. They are sociable birds detected by their noisy 'ping' call and by their low flight over the reeds with whirring wings.

SPARROWS, BUNTINGS AND FINCHES

Sparrows, buntings and finches are small birds, tending to be seen in family groups or larger flocks and generally feeding on seeds and small insects.

HOUSE SPARROW ▶

©MR

Although numbers have declined, the house sparrow remains one of Britain's best-known birds. At home in towns, villages and farm outbuildings, they often gather noisily in hedges at evening. In summer they enjoy a dust bath to get rid of unwanted pests.

©MR

◀ TREE SPARROW

Shyer and less common than house sparrows, the tree sparrow has a reddish-brown cap and a black patch on white cheeks, and habitually cocks its tail. Associated with hedgerows and woodland fringes, they are mainly found in the Midlands and across eastern and south-east England.

◀ REED BUNTING

In breeding plumage the male has a black head and bib, offset by a white 'moustache' and collar; females more closely resemble house sparrows and markings of both sexes are more muted in winter. Associated with reed fen and wetland habitat, they can resort to farmland in search of food.

©MR

©MR

YELLOWHAMMER ▶

A brightly coloured bunting of lowland heath and farmland hedgerows found across the UK, but is more common towards the south and east. It is most easily identified by its distinctive summer call of 'A little bit of bread and noooo cheese'.

©MR

CHAFFINCH ▲

The most common finch, it is ubiquitous throughout mainland Britain, the summer blue-grey cap and pinkish breast and cheeks setting the male apart from his mate. Naturally a woodland bird, the cheerful, chirruping song is an early sign of spring.

©MR

BRAMBLING ▶

Breeding in Eastern Europe, bramblings are winter visitors whose numbers are highly variable. Highly gregarious, they are likely to be seen in large flocks in beech woodlands feeding on beech mast; otherwise they mix with chaffinches, foraging for seeds in stubble fields.

◀ CROSSBILL

Typically encountered in noisy groups in the tree tops of coniferous woodland, established populations occur in the New Forest, Forest of Dean, Norfolk and the Scottish Highlands. Its specialised bill has overlapping tips to enable it to ferret out seeds from pine cones.

GREENFINCH ▼

Regular visitors to garden feeders, greenfinches are naturally a bird of open woodlands, parks and hedgerows and tend to gather in small flocks. They have a distinctive olive-green colouring with yellow wing and tail flashes.

BULLFINCH ▲

The male bullfinch has a handsomely rosy breast; both sexes have a black cap and white rump, particularly noted in flight. They are a bird of hedgerows, woodland edges and orchards. Due to their fondness in spring for fruit tree buds, they were once regarded as pests by orchard growers.

◀ GOLDFINCH

Its red face and bright colours make it immediately recognisable. They have fine beaks adapted to prise the seeds from thistles and teasels. After the breeding season, goldfinches gather in sociable groups in search of food; the flock not inappropriately being called a charm.

BLACKBIRD ▶

Males are black with a bright yellow bill, females are dark brown and the young, which are still fed by their parents after leaving the nest, are dark brown with speckled fronts. It is a common bird and its beautiful song is a feature of the dawn chorus throughout Britain.

Young blackbird bathing

◀ FIELDFARE

Winter visitors to Britain, fieldfares begin to arrive in October and increase in numbers as cold weather sets in on the continent. They have a bluish hue with chestnut back, dark tail and speckled breast and are often seen in large flocks feeding in open fields.

SONG THRUSH ▼

These are smaller and browner than mistle thrushes with smaller breast speckles. Its song repeats each separate 'phrase', sometimes more than twice, distinguishing it from the blackbird. Snails are a favourite food, their shells being smashed against an anvil-like stone with repeated flicks of the bird's head.

MISTLE THRUSH ▲

The largest member of the thrush family, it is known also as the storm cock for its habit of singing from a treetop perch in all weathers. Widespread but becoming uncommon, it eats berries – including mistletoe, yew and hawthorn – fruit, insects and earthworms.

REDWING ▼

Likely to be seen with fieldfares (but noticeably smaller) in farmland, parks and open grassland, redwings too are winter visitors to Britain. They are distinguished from song thrushes by red patches on their sides and under their wings as well as a prominent pale stripe above each eye.

STONECHAT ▼

Stonechats are sparrow-sized birds of heathland, uncultivated land and coastal areas in the southern and western counties of Britain. Its harsh call sounds like two stones being knocked together. Often seen in pairs, they perch on the tops of gorse bushes flicking their wings and flitting their tails.

Male

WREN ◀

One of Britain's smallest birds, the wren can be distinguished from other little brown birds by its habit of flicking its short cocked tail. It is likely to be spotted flitting in hedgerows and undergrowth in woods, parks and gardens on tiny whirring wings and calling in a high-pitched trill.

GOLDCREST ▶

Britain's tiniest bird, males have an orange crest while the female's is yellow. Breeding in coniferous woodland countrywide, they are continuously active, seeking out tiny insects in the undergrowth and in pine cones. They build an intricate nest suspended by basket-like handles under a conifer branch. Sadly, populations can be decimated in harsh winters.

SEDGE WARBLER ▼

Another summer visitor from Africa, the sedge warbler is typically found in thick vegetation and hedgerows near water and marsh, but not exclusively associated with sedge. It is a plump, small warbler with tawny brown back, pale buff under side and creamy eye stripe. Female cuckoos choose sedge warbler nests in which to lay their eggs more than any other victim.

Male

WHITETHROAT ▲

This is a migratory bird and summer visitor to Britain, favouring heathland, scrub and hedgerows. A sparrow-sized warbler, but with quite a long tail, both sexes have a white throat and chestnut wings. Males have a blue-grey cap and buff under parts. Whitethroats have a puppet-like vertical song flight.

WILLOW WARBLER and CHIFFCHAFF ◀

Hard to spot and virtually indistinguishable in appearance from each other, willow warblers and chiffchaffs are migrants. It is their distinctive calls that identify their presence and each is a welcome sign of spring. The willow warbler's song is a fluent series of gently descending notes. The call of the chiffchaff is a more monotonous series of high-pitched 'chiff-chaff, chiff-chaff, chiff-chaff' notes. Both species are fond of deciduous woods and parkland, particularly coppiced woodland.

Willow warbler

LARK, PIPIT, DIPPER AND WAGTAILS

SKYLARK ▶

Noted for its mellifluous warbling song, cascading as the bird ascends near vertically to become little more than a spec high in the sky, walkers on the downs, moors and open fields across the country are much more likely to hear a skylark than see one, particularly from February to June when breeding territories are being established and defended.

MEADOW PIPIT ▼

Common on the moors of northern and western Britain, meadow pipits are a small, streaky brown bird also found on rough open country elsewhere. When flushed into the air they give out a sharp 'pheet-pheet-pheet' call and in spring their territorial song is accompanied by a gliding descent.

YELLOW WAGTAIL ▶

This is a brightly coloured summer visitor from West Africa with yellowish green back and yellow breast and belly. They are most likely found on commons, pasture, wetland meadows and marshland, often feeding among grazing cattle and horses on insects stirred up by the animals' hoofs.

◀ PIED WAGTAIL

Also found alongside grazing animals feeding off flies and other insects, these beautifully marked black and white birds walk with a continuous, energetic flicking of their tails, darting to catch their prey. Seen across Britain, the females have a greyer back than the males.

DIPPER ▼

Dippers are at home in fast-flowing streams, mainly in upland areas. They bob and dip amongst the rocks and can walk upstream underwater in search of food such as water-beetles, insect larvae, minnows and other small fish. They have a conspicuous white bib against a dark, round body.

GREY WAGTAIL ▲

A brightly coloured wagtail, despite its name, they have bold yellow under parts, a blue-grey back and a long black tail with white edges. Resident in Britain and seen at all times of year, unlike the yellow wagtail, they patrol river banks in search of insect larvae, sometimes in the company of dippers in upland streams, but also seen in lowland streams, although rarely far from tumbling water.

GREAT SPOTTED WOODPECKER ▶

About the size of a blackbird, these are birds of mature woodland and well-wooded parks and gardens and are the most common and widespread of British woodpeckers.

GREEN WOODPECKER ▲

Living in well-wooded areas in England, Wales and southern Scotland, these birds are often seen on the ground in grassland and parkland looking for ants which they eat using their long, sticky tongue. They have a bouncy undulating flight and a distinctively loud, laughing call known as a yaffle.

LESSER SPOTTED WOODPECKER ▼

Our smallest woodpecker, little bigger than a sparrow, it tends to keep to deciduous woodland only and is less common than its great spotted relative. It does not breed in Scotland.

To advertise their presence, woodpeckers produce a drumming noise by giving repeated quick taps of their beak against a resonant piece of dead wood. The great spotted woodpecker makes a loud drumming noise, the lesser spotted woodpecker's drumming is quieter, but more prolonged, while the green woodpecker hardly drums at all.

NUTHATCH ▲

Nuthatches move headfirst down a tree trunk, the only British bird to do so. They resemble a small woodpecker, living in mature deciduous woodland, mainly eating hazel nuts, beech mast and acorns which they wedge into bark crevices and split with blows from their sharp beak.

TREECREEPER ▼

Well-camouflaged, treecreepers characteristically spiral their way up tree trunks using their small down-curved beaks to peck out insects from the bark. They are mousey brown above and white below. A shy woodland bird, they may congregate with flocks of tits in winter.

SWIFT, SWALLOW AND MARTINS

SWIFT ▶

Swifts feed, mate and even nap on the wing and spend more time in the air than any other bird. They are also one of the fastest fliers, achieving speeds of over 60 miles per hour. Swifts are dark all over but with a white chin patch. They have scythe-like wings and short forked tails, and were once known as 'devil birds' for their screeching flight around villages on late spring and summer evenings. So aerial are swifts by nature that they will never land on the ground or perch on overhead wires like swallows and martins.

Swifts, swallows and martins are all highly migratory birds and summer visitors to Britain. Swifts are usually the last to arrive, in late April, and the first to depart, in early August. Aerial in nature, these species have adapted to exploit different levels of air space and different insects taken on the wing. They tend to revisit the same nest site year after year.

HOUSE MARTIN ▼

House martins are excellent builders and construct a nest of mud, often against the roof eaves and soffits. They have blue-black upper parts, white undersides and a white rump. In autumn, house martins gather with swallows in larger groups, often perching on overhead wires before migrating south of the Equator.

©MR

▼ SWALLOW ▲

The swallow has a deeply forked tail and russet-coloured throat. They are agile and graceful in flight, often keeping close to the ground as they swoop and dart in pursuit of insects. Birds may arrive as early as March and, in favourable years, remain until October.

©MR

SAND MARTIN ▼

Smaller than house martins and swallows, sand martins lack the distinctive forked tail and are brown above and white below with a brown band across their chest. They mainly feed over water and nest in colonies, in deep burrows dug into riverbanks or sand and gravel pits.

©MR

STARLING

Starlings are highly opportunist and adaptable birds, equally at home in the city or countryside. Gregarious birds, in autumn and winter they can gather in spectacularly large groups at dusk, wheeling and diving as a single flock before dropping to roost together for warmth.

WOOD-PIGEON ▶

While their feral descendants have become a plague in towns and cities, wood-pigeons are no better regarded by farmers, for they voraciously feed on root and grain crops. They are the largest of Britain's doves and pigeons and display bold white upper wing bars in flight.

COLLARED DOVE ▼

More captivating is the collared dove, distinguished by a black collar. Also grain eaters, collared doves are now widespread but didn't appear in Britain until the 1950s.

RED GROUSE ▼

The red grouse relies almost entirely on heather and ling for food and is a game bird of upland moors. It has a distinctive 'kau kau g'bak g'bak' call and when startled, beats low over the heather on whirring wings. Moorlands are managed by rotational burning which encourages new heather growth for grouse.

PHEASANT ▼

Dotted across farmed countryside are small coverts and copses planted purposefully to provide cover for rearing game birds. Hidden within might be pens for young pheasant with feeders amongst the trees for adult birds. Although spending most of their time on the ground, pheasants roost up in the branches to avoid predators. They were originally brought from Eurasia during the Middle Ages and do well in the wild, even without the attentions of the gamekeeper.

GREY PARTRIDGE ▼

A farmland bird traditionally found in the lowland arable fields of eastern, central and southern England, partridges have a plump appearance with grey-brown plumage, barred chestnut markings and a chestnut face. They have a low, whirring flight interspersed with gliding on down-turned wings. Outside the breeding season they roost in groups called coveys, each facing outwards to watch for predators.

CROWS

JAY ▶

The jay is a woodland bird and the most colourful of the crows. It loves acorns, which it will bury together with beechnuts in readiness for the winter. The jay is responsible for helping oak woods to spread uphill. Nuts dropping off the tree will naturally roll downhill, but the jay will take them uphill too and those it forgets will sprout as new trees.

CARRION CROW ▼

As well as carrion, the crow is a notorious egg thief and will also take nestlings. It is an adaptable and clever bird and is at home in the city, the countryside and on the coast.

ROOK ▼

The sociable rook congregates in noisy rookeries, their ragged nests built at the top of tall trees. It is distinguishable from the crow by its white-grey bill. Essentially a farmland bird, they have a varied diet of worms, leatherjackets and other insect larvae, snails and grain.

CHOUGH

Pronounced 'chuff', and named after its 'k-chuf' call, the chough can be seen along the Welsh coastal cliffs and rather smaller than the crow, is distinguished by red legs and beak. It has spectacular aerobatic ability. Once common in Cornwall, it was said that King Arthur's spirit entered the bird when he died.

RAVEN ▼

The heavy-billed raven is our biggest crow; and is the world's largest perching bird. Seen on the hills and moors, carrion is a major food source although it will eat small mammals and young birds. The bird's habit of feeding off corpses left hanging on the gibbet led to it being regarded an ill omen.

©MR

MAGPIE ▲

The magpie is readily distinguished by a long tail and striking pied plumage. It has a reputation for raiding eggs and chicks of other birds and was traditionally regarded as an omen; seeing a pair foretold joy but a single bird was a sign of sorrow.

LAPWING ▶

Sometimes called a green plover from the dark green plumage on its back, the lapwing is often seen around ploughed fields and rough pastures, where it makes a nest scrape on the ground. Broad, rounded wings, a white belly and a prominent crest make it readily distinguishable, as does its familiar 'pee-wit' call, yet another name for the bird.

◀ DUNLIN

Probably Britain's commonest small wader, the Dunlin breeds mainly on the upland moors of Wales, northern England and Scotland and can be seen all year round in estuaries, appearing in sizeable flocks in winter. In summer breeding plumage dunlins have a black belly.

CURLEW ▶

Waders generally inhabit coastal marshes and estuaries, but the curlew can be found on moors too. The curlew is Britain's largest wader and breeds on the moorlands of north Wales, northern England and Scotland, then winters around the coast. Its size, long downward-curving bill and evocative 'coor-li' call clearly identify the curlew.

◀ WHIMBREL

Although breeding in Shetland and Orkney, the whimbrel is most likely to be seen as a passage migrant, visiting salt marshes and estuaries all round the coastline between May and September, and looks rather like a smaller curlew.

REDSHANK ▼

As its name implies, the redshank is identified by its long orange-red legs. A medium size wader (about 11 inches, 28cm, long), it also has an orange-red beak used to probe the soft mud of lake shores, water meadows, salt marsh and coastal mudflats for insects, worms and small shellfish.

GREY HERON ▲

Herons are patient, stealthy predators of fish, small mammals and amphibians. They can be found where there are ponds, along rivers and canals, lake and reservoir margins, wetlands and marsh, and estuarine coast. In flight herons display broad wings with head drawn back and legs trailing behind.

MALLARD ▼

The ubiquitous mallard is Britain's best-known duck. Drakes have a glossy green head; ducks are mottled brown. Both sexes have a blue-purple wing patch.

©SFI

Female

TUFTED DUCK ▼

Found on lakes, reservoirs and gravel pits across England and Scotland, both sexes have a recognisable 'tuft', which is longer in the drake. Males have a dark upper body and are white below; females are browner.

Male   ©MR

GOLDENEYE ▼

Although breeding in the Highlands, this medium-sized diving duck is more widely seen as a winter visitor from September through to March on lakes, reservoirs, estuaries and sheltered coasts. Males are black and white (note the white disk below the eye); females have brown heads and grey-brown upper body.

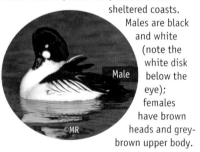

Male

©MR

SHOVELER ▼

Splendidly named, the shoveler is a surface-feeding duck that has a prominent, ungainly bill adapted to sifting water for insects and algae. It breeds in eastern and south-east counties and is more widespread in winter.

©MR

Male

©MR

TEAL ▲

The country's smallest duck is the teal, the male having a distinctive chestnut head and green eye-patch. Both sexes have a green and black wing patch; otherwise the female is mottled brown. Breeding on secluded rushy moorland, it is best seen in winter in wetland areas like the Somerset Levels and coastal estuaries.

©MR

Drake (left), duck (right)

EIDER ▲

Eider can be seen around the northern and eastern coasts of Britain. In Northumberland it is known as Cuddy's duck, so named after St Cuthbert gave it protection on Farne in the 7th century. They are sea ducks, eating mussels and other shellfish.

COOT ▼

The coot has a conspicuous white forehead and bill. On land its feet appear disproportionately large to its body and it walks rather inelegantly.

MOORHEN ▼

A little smaller than the coot, moorhens have a red beak and forehead and conspicuous white tail underparts. Its name derives from 'mere' hen and it is a common bird of lakes and ponds.

GREAT CRESTED GREBE ▼

Persecuted by the Victorians for its beautiful feathers, the great crested grebe is becoming more widespread again on inland waterways. Breeding everywhere except north-west Scotland, it can be seen around the coast during winter. Its double crest and ruff make it a striking bird and the courtship dance, in which the pair exchange presents of food, is a memorable sight.

GREYLAG GOOSE ▼

A resident goose, greylag numbers are swollen in winter in Scotland by visitors from Iceland. It is the largest of the native British geese and the ancestor of the farmyard goose. They are not popular with farmers whose grazing land and crops they invade. In flight, greylags have a pale leading wing edge.

BRENT GOOSE ▼

Brent geese overwinter on the tidal flats of the east and south coast of England. Identified by a dark head, neck and upper body with a white neck patch, Brent geese rarely stray far from the sea and the eel-grass on which they feed in winter.

CANADA GOOSE ▼

Canada geese, now widespread, were originally introduced in 1665 to St James' Park, London, from North America for King Charles II.

OYSTERCATCHER ▶

The noisy oystercatcher frequents river estuaries and shingle beaches. It is misnamed, for it uses its long orange bill to feed on worms and small shellfish.

RINGED PLOVER ▼

Ringed plovers nest on quieter beaches around the coastline as well as inland in sand and gravel pits. Although their eggs are well-camouflaged, adults

will feign a broken wing to distract gulls and other predators away from their scrape-nests when threatened.

CORMORANT ▶

Cormorants and shags are divers, and often are seen hanging their wings out to dry. Cormorants are larger than shags and have white cheek patches.

SHAG ▼

Shags are birds of sea-cliffs and rocky islands and, unlike the cormorant, are rarely seen inland or in estuaries. Shags are generally slimmer than cormorants and their flight tends to be faster, more direct and more graceful.

COMMON TERN ▲

Their long, forked tail and graceful flight has given rise to the nick-name 'swallow of the sea' and, typically, they are seen hovering above the water before plunging for a small fish or sand-eel. They have red legs and a red bill, usually with a black tip.

◀ KNOT

A stocky little blackbird-sized wader, knots are winter visitors to the larger estuaries around the coast, often in huge numbers feeding on the mud-flats for worms, small crabs and molluscs. In flight, dense flocks of knot show their pale undersides as a mass of white, which turns a darker flinty grey as they wheel together.

BLACK-HEADED GULL ▶

Normally a seabird, the black-headed gull will seek inland waters, and Barden Reservoir (Yorkshire Dales) boasts one of the North's largest breeding colonies. Their head is a chocolate brown, rather than black, in summer and turns white in the winter.

HERRING GULL ▶

Most seagulls are shore rather than seabirds, often moving far inland. Both the herring and black-headed gulls have become efficient scavengers and a nuisance in many towns and cities. Its raucous yelping wail is a common seaside sound.

RAZORBILL ▼

Razorbills and guillemots are members of the auk family. Both are expert divers and have short, stubby wings, as much adapted for swimming as flying, and spend their life largely on the oceans, coming to land only to breed. The razorbill is the emblem of the Pembrokeshire National Park.

◀ KITTIWAKE

A slender gull nesting in cliff colonies, the kittiwake is rarely found inland and takes its name from its call. Winters are mostly spent out at sea, so the breeding season is the best time to see it.

FULMAR ▼

Fulmars are related to albatrosses. They fly low over the sea, gliding with wings held stiffly and ride the rising air currents superbly at their sea-cliff nesting colonies. Their tubular nostrils identify them, closer to, from similar size gulls.

◀ GUILLEMOT

Guillemots, like razorbills, breed in colonies on narrow cliff ledges but they make no nest. Their eggs are pear-shaped and so are less susceptible to roll off the ledge. Guillemots have brown upper parts and a pointed bill; razorbills have a thicker bill and black upper body.

©MR

BUZZARD ▲

The commonest large raptor countrywide is the buzzard, which has a wingspan of around four feet and is noted for its extremely keen eyesight. They patrol open hillsides and wooded valleys, soaring on thermals in slow, wide circles as they watch for prey.

LITTLE OWL ▶

©MR

The little owl is a bird of open country in England and Wales, is Britain's smallest owl and is day-flying, although it flies by night too, and hunts chiefly at dawn and dusk. It is most likely to be seen sitting on a vantage point such as a telegraph pole or wire.

©MR

RED KITE ▶

The red kite is slightly larger than the buzzard but its forked tail and angled wings distinguish it. Its range is expanding once again in mid-Wales, and introduced populations in central-southern and northern England and southern Scotland are well established and growing.

SPARROWHAWK ▼

A small hawk, the sparrowhawk has short and rounded wings for fast, manoeuvrable flight amongst trees to hunt small birds. It often patrols the woodland fringe and relies on surprise attack to take its prey. The alarm calls of small birds may give away its presence.

©SFI

Male

©MR

Female

KESTREL ▲

The kestrel is a small falcon with pointed wings and long tail, noted for its hovering flight. This it achieves by flying forward as fast as the wind is pushing it back. Once it has spotted a mouse or vole, it will drop vertically, talons outstretched upon its prey. It is found throughout Britain.

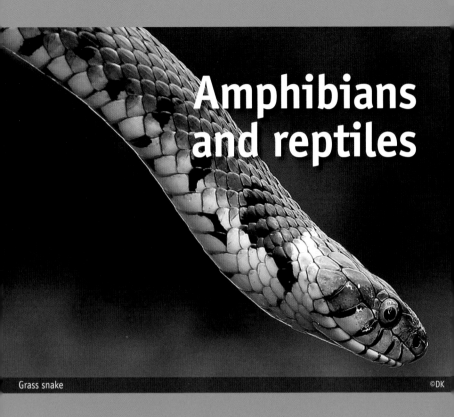

Amphibians and reptiles

Grass snake ©DK

Herpetology is the study of amphibians and reptiles. Both groups are cold-blooded, and unlike birds and mammals, have no internal mechanism for regulating body temperature. During cold weather, their body temperature drops and they become torpid. On sunny days, they are active after basking in the warming sun, but seek shade when it is too hot. Winter forces a dormant state, their metabolism slowing with decreasing temperature, a different technique to mammals that live off stored body fat during hibernation.

Amphibian derives from the Greek and means living on land and water. Hatching from eggs generally laid in water they begin life as tadpoles, breathing through gills. Approaching adulthood they develop legs and primitive lungs, but retain the ability to absorb oxygen directly through their skin. Reptiles on the other hand have an impervious scaly skin and are air-breathing from birth. Female adders and grass snakes lay eggs, while the young of slow worms and common lizards are born in egg sacs that break during or soon after birth.

The seven species of British amphibian include frogs and toads, as well as newts, which belong to the salamander family. Frogs and toads lay their eggs as spawn that floats in the water, a single toad being able to produce up to 7,000 eggs at a time. Newts lay up to 300 individual eggs in the folds of underwater plant leaves, a process that can take many hours.

There are six species of native reptile, all favouring dry heathlands – a rapidly declining habitat. Some, like the adder, can be found throughout mainland Britain while the sand lizard and smooth snake tend to live only in the southern counties. There are one or two places where all six can be found, such as Wareham Forest in Dorset. All reptiles have teeth, which are replaced throughout life, and they will slough or shed their skin during the course of the year.

COMMON FROG ▶

The common frog is widespread throughout Britain. It has a smooth, moist skin, which generally ranges in colour from olive-green to brown, but can be highly variable with individual irregular markings. They favour damp habitats and breed in freshwater ponds, laying their spawn in large clumps. Frogs eat slugs and snails and overwinter at the bottom of pools, absorbing oxygen through their skin.

◀ COMMON TOAD

Reaching more than 3 inches (8cm), the common toad is larger and bulkier than a frog and has a rough, warty skin, which is generally dark and spotted. Toads feed on insects, slugs and snails. They crawl rather than leap and live largely on dry land, only returning to water – often to the same large ponds used for breeding year after year – to lay long, double strings of spawn often laced around reed stems.

NATTERJACK TOAD ▼

Much rarer is the smaller natterjack toad, found only in the coastal dunes of north-west England and the Solway coast. Reintroductions are taking place on the sandy heaths of East Anglia and southern England where it once occurred naturally. Breeding in warm, shallow ponds between dunes that often dry up during summer, their spawn is laid in a single strand. By day they will shelter in burrows, emerging at night to feed on insects.

SMOOTH NEWT ▲

The most widespread of the newts is the common or smooth newt. Up to 4 inches (10cm) long and having a smooth, soft skin and long, flattened tail, it is olive brown with an orange belly, the male developing a dorsal crest during the breeding season. They generally hide amongst leaf litter and under stones, emerging to feed at night, but return to pools to breed. The spawn is laid as single eggs, each wrapped separately in a leaf of pond weed by the female. Unlike frog and toad tadpoles, which develop hind legs first, the forelegs appear initially in newt tadpoles.

GREAT CRESTED NEWT ▶

The rarest and largest of the British newts is the great crested newt, which may grow up to 7 inches (17.5cm) long. It has a warty skin and develops a prominent, jagged dorsal crest and prefers to breed in deep pools containing plenty of weed.

Female (above) and male

ADDER ▼

The adder, Britain's only poisonous snake (rarely fatal to adults), only bites if provoked. Growing up to 2 feet (60cm) long they have a black zigzag marking down their back and a keen sense of smell, 'tasting' the air with their tongue to find their prey. The four jaw bones can move independently, enabling them to swallow prey larger than the width of their head. They are found across Britain in a range of open habitats such as moorland, downland and heathland.

GRASS SNAKE ▲

Growing up to 3 feet long (90cm), the grass snake is the largest of Britain's snakes. Usually olive coloured, it has darker bars along its flanks and a cream collar. Grass snakes like damp habitats and prefer being near water, their diet consisting of fish and amphibians. They lay up to 40 eggs, often under decaying vegetation to keep them warm.

SMOOTH SNAKE ▶

Similar in size to adders, but more slender, smooth snakes are brown or grey-coloured with a double row of dorsal spots that are sometimes joined to appear striped. Quite rare, they are restricted to heaths between east Dorset and west Surrey, and are hard to spot for they spend much of their time underground.

COMMON LIZARD ▼

The common lizard is shy, although is most likely seen basking in a sunny spot on heathland or dry open country; but if alarmed will dart into undergrowth or a rocky crevice. If not quite quick enough to evade a predator, they can discard their tail to confuse it and then make good their escape. Adults grow to 6 inches (15cm) long and, like the adder, the female retains her eggs and gives live birth to as many as eleven young.

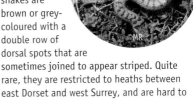

SLOW WORM ▲

Although looking like a snake, the slow worm is actually a legless lizard and, like many other lizards, may shed its tail to escape capture. They have shiny skin and the colour varies from grey to brick red. Females have a fine, dark stripe along their back. They can grow up to 18 inches (45cm) long and are quite common throughout Britain, although they tend to hide away under logs, stones, in crevices and thick vegetation.

Insects

Purple emperor

©MR

'Insect' derives from the Latin meaning cut into sections, referring to their three body parts termed head, thorax and abdomen. All insects have six legs and are usually, but not always winged. Their external skeleton affords protection from predators as armour, but effectively limits growth and the majority of insects progress through four distinct forms during their life-cycle; egg, larva, pupa (called a chrysalis for butterflies and moths) and adult. However some groups, such as dragonflies, grasshoppers and earwigs have only three stages, the eggs hatching into nymphs, which moult and gradually metamorphose into the winged adult. Most insects are land dwellers, although a few live in water like the boatman, which uses its long rear legs like paddles, while others have an aquatic larval stage before emerging to fly.

Britain's biggest insect is the death's head hawkmoth, which has a wingspan of over 5 inches (125mm) and emits a loud squeaking sound if disturbed. Unusually it will raid beehives for honey. The largest land insect is the stag beetle at up to 3 inches (75mm) long. In dramatic contrast, with a wingspan of only one tenth of an inch (about 2.5mm), is the fairy fly, a tiny parasitic wasp that lays eggs in those of other insects. Even smaller is the hardly visible flea beetle, which measures just one thirtieth of an inch (less than 1mm).

While many people have a general and often-irrational distaste or even fear of flying and creeping crawlies, some species engender a more positive and even endearing reaction. Ladybirds and butterflies have long been anthropomorphised in children's books; a mother ladybird cares for the hero in Roald Dahl's tale *James and the Giant Peach* while fairies are closely linked with butterflies. Many moths, dragonflies and damselflies are regarded as pretty, and although we go out of our way to avoid wasps and hornets, busy bees are looked upon with fondness.

BRIMSTONE ▼

The brimstone favours open woodland and scrubland where its caterpillars feed on buckthorn. This is the 'butter-coloured fly' that gave rise to the generic name. Males are a brighter yellow than females. Brimstones hibernate as adults in winter, often amongst ivy, and may be seen on the wing early in the year on sunny days. Fresh adults emerge in August.

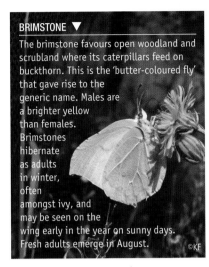
©KF

©KF

COMMA ▲

The comma is recognised by its jagged wing outline, on the dark underside of which is a small white 'C' or comma shape. When resting, it has the appearance of an old leaf, a camouflage strategy for winter hibernation. Seen across England and Wales, the caterpillar feeds on hops and nettles.

SMALL TORTOISESHELL ▼

Stinging nettle is the main food plant of the small tortoiseshell caterpillar and the butterfly is distributed throughout Britain. A recent decline in numbers is perhaps due to a parasitic fly, which lays its eggs amongst the nettles. Eaten whole by the caterpillars, the larval fly develops within the host, slowly consuming it.

©SFI

PAINTED LADY ▼

The painted lady is a migrant flying from northern Africa in late spring and, in a good year, may produce a second generation. Thistles are the main caterpillar food plant.

©KF

PEACOCK ▼

The large eye-like markings on the peacock's wings are unmistakable and are a defence strategy that helps protect it from hungry birds. Eggs are laid in batches on the underside of young stinging nettles and look out for the silken 'tent' the caterpillars make in which the group feeds.

RED ADMIRAL ▼

The red admiral is also a migrant arriving in Britain to breed from southern Europe. Adults nectar on buddleia and sedum, commonly seen in parks and gardens. The caterpillars feed on stinging nettles.

©KF

©KF

BUTTERFLIES

LARGE WHITE ▶

The largest of the 'cabbage whites' with a wingspan of 2½ inches (63mm), they have black forewing tips and the female has two black spots on each forewing. Their caterpillars feed on cabbages and Brussels sprouts.

Male

MEADOW BROWN ▶

Perhaps Britain's commonest butterfly, it is seen from mid-June through to autumn in most types of grassy areas from hillsides to verges and open woodland. It flies even in dull or damp weather. Both sexes are darker brown above, grey-brown below. Females have more orange on their upper sides.

GATEKEEPER or HEDGE BROWN ▶

Find the gatekeeper along verges, hedgerows and woodland rides from July through to autumn. It is smaller than the meadow brown with stronger brownish-orange upper wing patches.

◀ ORANGE TIP

The orange tip, also a 'white', favours hedgerows and woodland fringes. Only the male has orange on the forewings; females have the black tips and a forewing black spot. Garlic mustard is the main caterpillar food plant.

Male

◀ MARBLED WHITE

Another grassland species and found in the Midlands and southern England, its highly distinctive black and creamy white markings easily identify the marbled white. On the wing in July and August, it has a rather slow flight and adults like to nectar on thistles, knapweed and scabious.

◀ SPECKLED WOOD

Predominantly dark brown, with a variable number of pale yellow patches or spots on their upper wings, they are found in woodland glades and overgrown hedgerows, preferring dappled sunlight and shade. Unusually, it can overwinter both as a pupa and caterpillar.

COMMON BLUE ▶

The common blue is the most widespread of British blues with a wingspan of about 1½ inches (35mm). Females are brown – as in many blues – with a dusting of blue; both sexes have similar undersides. They inhabit open grasslands, particularly limestone and chalk downs, laying eggs amongst birdsfoot trefoil. Emerging in June and with two generations a year, sometimes three in the South, they may be seen into October.

Male ©MR

©KF

◀ SILVER-WASHED FRITILLARY

Britain's largest fritillary (wingspan – 3 inches, 75mm), males are bright orange-brown with black markings above, while females have a duller brown background. The eponymous silver-wash is displayed on the underside of the hind wing. A strong flyer, it likes sunny woodland fringes and open ground nearby where dog violets flourish – its caterpillar food plant. Adults can be seen in July.

Male

SIX-SPOT BURNET ▶

One of the commonest of the day-flying moths, the six-spot burnet has vivid red spots to warn birds of its horrible taste. It is slightly poisonous, feeding on birdsfoot trefoil from which it absorbs hydrogen cyanide. They can be seen from June to August in grasslands, woodland clearings and around the coast.

©KF

HUMMINGBIRD HAWKMOTH ▼

Also a day-flyer, the hummingbird hawkmoth is an increasingly regular visitor from Africa and, when influxes are large, may be seen across Britain. Sometimes mistaken for a small humming bird, they hover at flowers to drink nectar through a long proboscis.

©MR

ELEPHANT HAWKMOTH ▲

Although a night flier, the elephant hawkmoth is particularly beautiful, having soft pink and olive coloured markings. With a wingspan of around 2½ inches (60mm), it is an impressive sight and may be spotted around dusk, from May to July, feeding on honeysuckle. Its fully grown caterpillar bears some resemblance to an elephant's trunk, hence the moth's name.

DRAGONFLIES AND DAMSELFLIES

Dragonflies tend to fly strongly and rest with wings open and may be seen well away from water, while damselflies stay close to water, rest with wings closed and tend to be weaker in flight. Although found countrywide, the Broads is a particularly rewarding place for spotting dragonflies and damselflies, with the National Park adopting the Norfolk hawker for its logo.

©SFI

COMMON BLUE DAMSELFLY ▲

Abundant throughout Britain on ponds, lakes, canals and rivers, the common blue is distinguished from other blue and black damselflies by the broad banding along its body. It flies from April to October.

©SFI

SOUTHERN HAWKER DRAGONFLY ▲

On the wing from June to October, the southern hawker breeds in overgrown ponds and is distributed across the Midlands and southern England and Wales. It can be seen glinting in the sunshine of woodland rides where it hunts.

©MR

EMPEROR DRAGONFLY ▲

Just over 3 inches (78mm) long, the emperor dragonfly has a bulky appearance. Both sexes have a green thorax, but males have a bright blue abdomen while the female's is greener. Its range is increasing northwards but it is most commonly associated with well-vegetated, large ponds and lakes in Wales and the southern half of England.

LARGE RED DAMSELFLY ▼

Widespread and common on still or slow-flowing bodies of water, the large red is one of the first species of damselfly to emerge in spring, its flight season being from April to September.

©MR

©MR

COMMON DARTER DRAGONFLY ▲

A small dragonfly, only 1½ inches (40mm) long, the common darter may be on the wing until November and is the latest flying of British species. Mature males are a bright orange-red, females are yellow-brown.

HONEY BEE ▲

Within a honey bee community, sterile female workers fly out to gather nectar, which is made into honey and stored in wax cells each containing an egg. They are responsible for feeding the growing larvae on honey and pollen and tending the queen. Male drones ventilate the hive to maintain temperature; they also fertilise a new queen. Unlike other bees, female honey bees overwinter as a colony, huddling together for warmth and living off stored honey. At the height of summer a hive may contain 50,000 bees and can produce 60lb of honey during the year, flying 55,000 miles to collect nectar for just one pound of honey. Only the female bees sting, a last resort defensive action since they die when the barbed stinger is ripped out as she flies away.

WASP ▲

The familiar common wasp, like the honey bee, is a social animal and builds paper nests from chewed wood, enlarging them as the colony grows. Again only females sting, to paralyse or kill prey, but can make unprovoked attacks on people, particularly in late summer. Despite their reputation, they are great pest controllers and feed largely upon other insects. Many solitary wasps are parasitic, laying eggs inside insect larvae, with others parasitising plants, for example the oak apple gall wasp.

RED-TAILED and WHITE-TAILED BUMBLEBEES ▼

Britain has 25 species of bumblebee. They are vital pollinators of farmed fruit and vegetables and the decline in bumblebee numbers over recent years is a concern to growers. The red-tailed variety has a black abdomen and a bright orange-red tail tip. The white-tailed has a yellow band across the thorax and on the abdomen and has a white tail.

HOVERFLY ▼

There are about 250 different species in Britain and many of them mimic the black and yellow warning stripes of the bees, bumblebees and wasps, but are completely harmless, feeding off nectar. Their hovering ability and manoeuvrability are amazing.

BEETLES

Beetles have two pairs of wings, although the forewings have developed into a protective case over the flight wings. There are almost 4,000 different kinds in Britain.

LADYBIRD ▼

The endearing ladybird comes in many different guises and there are around 44 separate species in Britain. Some are plain and dull coloured, but others have spots, which can range from two to twenty two. The gardener's friend, both grubs and adults hunt aphids and a single ladybird can consume fifty a day.

©DK

COMMON COCKCHAFER ▼

In its larval life stage grubs usually live for three years underground before pupating in early spring. The adult cockchafer first appears in May, giving it the name May Bug.

©DK

SHIELDBUGS ▶

Superficially similar to beetles, shieldbugs are often brightly coloured in greens and browns and are named for their shield-shaped backs. Many can emit pungent fluid when alarmed, giving them the name stink bug. There are about 30 different species in Britain.

Female

©MR

STAG BEETLE ▲

This is Britain's largest beetle but individuals can vary in size from around 1½-3 inches (35-75mm). Females are slightly smaller than males and lack the 'antlers' that give the beetle its name, which are not horns but enlarged mandibles. They are scarce but might be seen in the woodlands of south and south-east England, only in the summer months. The sole purpose of the adult's life is to mate and they are relatively short-lived, the males dying soon after mating and the females after egg laying.

©MR

GREEN TIGER BEETLE ▲

This shiny metallic and spotted beetle is a carnivore. Tiger beetles are among the fastest-running insects and can achieve speeds of over 5mph – apparently equivalent to 480mph in human terms. They are about ½ inch (12mm) long and widespread on bare waste ground, on sandy heathlands and dunes.

©DK

Is it going to rain?

A gathering storm near Bolam Lake, Northumberland   ©DK

Britain's climate is remarkably mild for its latitude, tempered by the Atlantic Ocean and Gulf Stream. Ocean temperatures fluctuate considerably less than those of continental landmasses and air warmed in contact with water brought by the Gulf Stream enables palms to grow on Scotland's north-western coast.

But, while extremes of temperature are unusual, rain and wind are not, for the mid-Atlantic is a breeding ground for cyclonic depressions that spiral anticlockwise towards Britain. Warm, moisture-laden air from the south meets denser, cold Arctic air to form weather fronts, logically termed warm (where warmer air is replacing colder at ground level) or cold. Falling temperature and increasing air pressure are associated with a cold front, the opposite being true for a warm front. While both can bring rain, the passage of a warm front generally leaves warmer, drier conditions in its wake.

Terrain is also a factor. Driven north and east by prevailing winds, moist air is forced upward by Britain's mountains and cooled.

Water vapour condenses as cloud and rain upon the western and northern slopes, leaving the eastern lee generally drier.

Settled weather and clear skies are associated with anticyclones, large, slow moving areas of high pressure. Rotating slowly clockwise, they can bring a heatwave in summer that often ends in thunderstorms, but in winter, there can be prolonged heavy frost, with morning fog persisting if there is no wind.

Despite its moderation, Britain's weather is highly changeable. Overcast skies and heavy rain can quickly dissipate to leave a glorious day and conditions in adjacent valleys can be contrasting. Variability is greatest near mountains and the coast, where abruptly rising ground holds back or collects cloud, deflects airflow or traps the heat of the sun.

Weather patterns have an overall predictability, but the detail remains chaotic and despite sophisticated computer modelling and vast amounts of data, detailed forecasting remains an inexact science.

CLOUDS

Clouds are composed of tiny water droplets or ice crystals, formed when moist air rises and cools. They are classified according to base altitude: below 6,500 feet – low, up to 20,000 feet – alto and above 20,000 feet – cirro. Cloud at ground level is known as mist or fog.

CUMULONIMBUS ▼

In hot weather, the cloud tower can rise to high altitudes, creating the typical 'anvil' shape of cumulonimbus or thundercloud. Potentially holding thousands of tons of water, they produce very heavy rain or hailstorms.

©MR

©DK

CUMULUS ▲

Warm ground causes air to rise by convection, the moisture condensing to form billowing white heaps of cumulus at low altitudes, but which dissipate quickly if caught in a downdraft. In large areas of clear sky they are generally fair-weather clouds.

CIRROCUMULUS ▼

Fluffy, fragmented clouds at mid altitudes are known as altocumulus and, although not generally bringing rain, can indicate a later storm. At higher altitudes such clouds can form into cirrocumulus, sometimes called a mackerel sky. Reflecting a low sun, it can produce a dramatic sky at the beginning or end of the day.

©MR

CIRRUS ▲

Wispy cirrus clouds form at high altitudes and are composed entirely of ice crystals. Known as mare's tails, they can signify an approaching front. Cirrostratus is a thin, veil-like cloud, generally extending across the sky and sometimes giving the sun or moon a halo. Such clouds often precede precipitation, particularly if accompanied by lower cloud.

©DK

STRATUS ▲

Stratus, meaning layered, is a low level, murky cloud which can bring light rain and drizzle. Altostratus is a large thin mid-level layer veiling a watery sun and can indicate an advancing front, and may thicken to a mass of dark grey nimbostratus that can bring persistent and often heavy rain.

Daily forecasts first appeared in 1860 in *The Times*, provided by the British Meteorological Office under Robert Fitzroy, who had captained *HMS Beagle* during Darwin's circumnavigation.

In the past, Man relied solely on his observation of the sky and the way plants and animals behaved. Accumulated experience was handed down in rhyme or linked to certain dates and inevitably was not that reliable.

Seaweed and pinecones were traditionally used in foretelling the weather. But while a piece of seaweed might well become slimy when humidity is high, an open pinecone is not a reliable indicator of dry weather. However, dandelions close when it clouds over and scarlet pimpernels close when humidity increases.

High-flying swallows are probably chasing insects on updrafts of warm air, which is a sign of stable, fine weather. On the other hand, cows lying down are more likely to be simply chewing the cud or resting rather than waiting for rain. But bees do not like the wet weather and will remain by the hive if rain is on its way.

'*Red sky at night, sailor's delight, red sky in morning, sailor's warning*' has its roots in the bible (Matthew 16:2-3) and often holds true. British weather usually comes from the west, so a clear evening sky heralds fine weather, while a red morning sky can be caused by high cirrus clouds at the leading edge of a front. Similarly, the high wispy clouds of '*Mare's tails and mackerel scales*' indicate an approaching front.

Many ditties refer to the moon. Cloudless night-time skies in winter allow the heat of the day to dissipate quickly and, without a breeze, '*clear moon, frost soon*' was often a reliable predictor of a cold snap. The tiny ice crystals in thin, high cloud can refract the light of the sun or moon to create a soft surrounding radiance, and '*Halo around the sun or moon, rain or snow soon*' foretells the possibility of an advancing front with its precipitation.

©DK

Rainbows can be striking phenomena and are caused by the refraction and reflection of sunlight through droplets of moisture in the air. They always appear in the opposite direction to the sun and in the afternoon often materialise after a heavy shower. However, '*Rainbow in the morning gives fair warning*' indicates rain in the west and generally heading your way.

Some sayings associated with special days; Candlemas Day (2nd February – a double winter), St Swithin's Day (15th July – forty days' rain) and Michaelmas Day (29th September – snow at Christmas), are pure superstition and have become established because people only remember the years on which the prophesy was fulfilled.

Short-term area meteorological forecasts can be reasonably accurate, but a reliable long-range prognosis is a much greater challenge. In Wales they say '*When you can see the hills, it's going to rain; when you can't see the hills, it is raining!*'

©DK

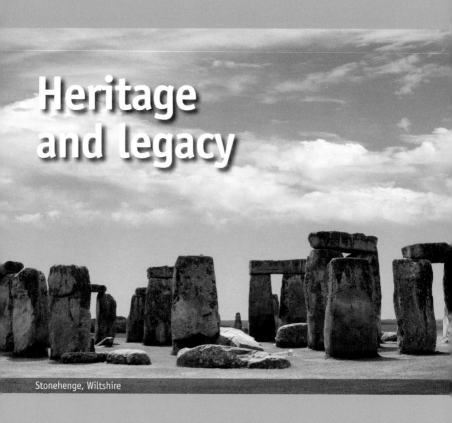

Heritage and legacy

Stonehenge, Wiltshire

RELICS FROM PREHISTORY

Constructed of wood and thatch, most prehistoric buildings have disappeared almost without trace. But startling exceptions are the 5,500 year-old stone-built farmsteads on Papa Westray (Orkney Islands) and Skara Brae (Mainland Orkney). More commonly surviving is communal architecture; monumental stone and earthwork structures that can still dominate their landscape and, although the purpose of many is now conjecture, they offer an enigmatic link with a distant past.

Amongst the earliest enduring structures are causewayed enclosures from 3500BC. Some 70 have been identified, mostly located on southern England's chalklands and predominantly occupying hilltop sites, as at Combe Hill above Eastbourne. Concentric banked ditches broken by multiple causeway entrances surround the enclosures, which are thought to have served a ceremonial purpose, perhaps for communal seasonal gatherings. Funerary monuments first appeared during the Stone Age, adopting many forms such as long and round barrows (tumuli), passage graves and portal tombs (cromlechs, quoits and dolmens). Used over an extended period, they often embodied multiple chambers within a single mound, like Stoney Littleton Long Barrow (Somerset). Many portal tombs have lost their covering to reveal slab or monolithic uprights supporting a massive capstone such as at Tinkinswood (Vale of Glamorgan).

Roughly circular and defined by a bank and internal ditch, henges defined a ritual space apart from daily life and, like Stonehenge, were often associated with a stone circle. Their construction continued into the Bronze Age and an astronomical alignment is often claimed. Avebury's outer circle (Wiltshire) has a diameter of 1,088 feet (331.7m) and is Britain's largest, but many smaller and equally impressive examples exist.

Thought to have been a ceremonial avenue and often related to nearby features such as henges or barrows, cursuses are bound by parallel banks and outer ditch. The longest is in Dorset and runs for six miles at the foot of Cranborne Chase.

CUP AND RING MARKS ▼

Perhaps the most enigmatic traces of ancient Man are the cup and ring carvings found on boulders and outcrops across the moorland hills of Northumberland and on Ilkley Moor (North Yorkshire). These mysterious marks are variously dated to the Neolithic, Bronze and Iron ages.

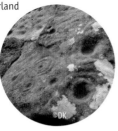
©DK

HUT CIRCLES ▼

The earliest built dwellings were roundhouses and some, built upon low, dry stone walls, have survived as hut circles, the entrance often dog-legged to keep out the weather. Dartmoor and Anglesey are amongst the best places to see them.

©DK

BROCHS ▼

Found only in Scotland, brochs date from the Iron Age. These dry stone constructions have squat, circular towers within a stout outer wall. Inside a staircase led to upper rooms. Occupying a good defensive site, the impressive Carloway broch measures 30 feet (9m) high by 50 feet (15m) wide.

©SFI
Carloway Broch, Isle of Lewis

MENHIRS ▼

Menhirs or standing stones occur either singly or in groups such as the Devil's Arrows near Boroughbridge (North Yorkshire). At over 25 feet tall, Britain's largest is in Rudstone's churchyard (Yorkshire Wolds). Those at Stenness may have been erected more than 5,000 years ago.

Stenness, Mainland Orkney   ©SFI

HILL FORTS ▼

Defending settlements with one or more embanked ditches topped with a stockade began during the late Bronze Age and continued until the Romans arrived in AD 43. Often exploiting hilltop geography, they varied considerably in size, Maiden Castle (Dorset) being the largest in Britain. Over 2,000 have been identified, but not all were permanently settled or wholly defensive.

©MR
Cissbury Ring, West Sussex

EMBANKED DITCHES

Linear embanked ditches were used to mark or defend territorial boundaries. The 4th-century Bokerley Ditch in Dorset, thrown up by the Roman-British to impede the Saxon advance, and Offa's Dyke, built to keep the Welsh out of Mercia in the 8th century, are two still-impressive examples.

MOTTE AND BAILEY ▶

A new age in architecture dawned with the Norman Conquest. The primary motivation was to consolidate military gains and maintain subjugation. The early Norman castles consisted of a simple wooden tower or keep upon a raised, earth mound overlooking a courtyard fortified by a palisaded earthwork - the motte and bailey. Fine examples are Castle Stede at Melling (Lancashire) and Pilsbury Castle (Derbyshire).

Castle Stede

Chepstow Castle

BORDER CASTLES ▲

Many motte and baileys were soon rebuilt in stone. Extensions and improvements reflected their strategic importance, the owner's status and developments in the engines of war. Of particular note are the border castles between England and Wales – Goodrich (EH, Herefordshire), Chepstow, Monmouth, White Castle, Skenfrith and Grosmont (all Cadw, Wales).

PELES ▼

In the borderland between Scotland and England, however, lawlessness persisted through the centuries and many tower houses and peles, such as Preston Tower at Ellingham (Northumberland), were built.

MANORIAL CASTLES ▼

Social ambition as well as unrest encouraged even minor knights to seek licences to crenellate and many medieval manor houses were moated or equipped with gatehouses and battlements such as Baddesley Clinton (NT, Warwickshire) and Oxburgh Hall (NT, Norfolk). By the 15th century, internal conflict lessened and castles began to incorporate more comfortable accommodation. Like Alnwick Castle (Northumberland) many embraced the Renaissance with luxurious apartments, banqueting halls and gardens; the concept of a palace had arrived.

Oxburgh Hall

MARTELLO TOWERS ▼

The threat of French invasion prompted a series of coastal forts during the 19th century in response to Napoleon's ambitions. Martello towers were built along the south and east coast and 47 of the original 103 survive.

Moy Castle, Loch Buie, Mull

SAXON CHURCH ▷

Little remains of Saxon architecture, for although many churches were founded, those in stone have largely been rebuilt and often only isolated features remain, such as characteristic long and short stonework. Notable exceptions are the churches at Earls Barton (Northamptonshire), Escombe (County Durham) and Steyning (pictured).

St Botolph's Church, Steyning, East Sussex

Church of St Peter and St Paul, Lavenham

THE PARISH CHURCH ▲

Many village and parish churches were founded before the 15th century and often display a multiplicity of architectural styles. Usually the oldest building in the village, the church was a focus of medieval life and can hold clues to the area's history. Local prosperity was reflected in the proportions and lavishness of the decoration, East Anglia's 'wool' churches being fine examples – such as Lavenham –, whilst the fabric of its construction can reveal the area's underlying geology.

HOLY WELLS ▷

Holy wells often adopted ancient Pagan sites, where water rising mysteriously out of the ground was revered for its purity, curative powers or the fact it persisted throughout drought. Those at St Non's and Llanllawer (pictured) in Pembrokeshire, for example, are said to cure eye complaints. Christianisation often attributed such wells to an early saint and many shrines became a place of pilgrimage.

NORMAN CHURCH ▽

Despite their often-brutal rule, the Normans were both cultured and religious, traits that found expression in a surge of religious foundation, construction and rebuilding that continued throughout the medieval period.

Norman arch of St Helen's Church, Overton, Lancashire ©DK

PRIORIES AND ABBEYS ▽

The tradition of communal monasticism begun by the Celts with the foundation of Iona, Lindisfarne and Whitby continued under the Saxons. The golden age, however, dawned with the Normans. Surviving priories and abbeys were rebuilt and many more were founded together with generous endowments of land for their support. Favoured locations were remote riverside settings and great monasteries like Fountains, Rievaulx (both in North Yorkshire) and Glastonbury (Somerset) flourished until the Dissolution under Henry VIII from 1536-41. Today they lie largely in ruins, although sometimes the abbey church has survived as the parish church, as at Beaulieu, Hampshire.

Lindisfarne Priory

Blickling Hall

Stourhead (NT, Wiltshire)

COUNTRY HOUSE ▲

Greater stability during the Tudor period saw the transition from fortified, functional dwellings to the more comfortable and luxuriously decorated country house. Wealthy landowners began demonstrating their status in grand buildings, some, like Lacock Abbey (NT, Wiltshire) and Studley Royal (NT, North Yorkshire) were centred on the former monastic estates which passed into secular hands at the Dissolution. Others such as Blickling Hall (NT, Norfolk) grew out of manorial estates.

COUNTRY ESTATE ▲

Like the grand houses, the country estates that surrounded them evolved over time. Their origins lay in the great Saxon and Norman hunting forests and the concept of a deer park persisted through the centuries, several, like Woburn Abbey (Bedfordshire) and Lyme Park (NT, Cheshire) remaining today. The outlying tenant farms, whose income supported the estate, saw change too, particularly during the agricultural improvements of the 18th century when many model farms were established as at Shugborough (NT, Staffordshire) and Wimpole Hall (NT, Cambridgeshire). The parkland and formal gardens more immediate to the house altered as well, from the formal Renaissance design like that of the restored gardens at Kenilworth Castle (EH, Warwickshire) to the more natural visions of Henry Hoare II (Stourhead) and the great landscape designer Capability Brown. He worked on or influenced hundreds of estates up and down the country, including Chatsworth (Derbyshire) and Harewood House (West Yorkshire).

Broadway Tower, Worcestershire

FOLLY ▲

Follies and commemorations litter the landscape. Follies range from heaps of stones conjuring an ancient, Romantic ruin such as Mow Cop castle (Cheshire) to elegant classic temples like those above Rievaulx Abbey (North York Moors), and although often purely decorative, some served as summer houses or lookouts such as Broadway Tower (Cotswolds). Queen Victoria's jubilees spawned a host of commemorative structures, but others remember British heroes like Wellington (Stratfield Saye, Hampshire) and Cook (Great Ayton, North York Moors).

VILLAGE SIGN ▼

There is usually a story behind each village sign, which often depict elements of the settlement's history. At Poynings, nestled in the South Downs near Brighton, the Devil represents the village's proximity to the famous Devil's Dyke dry valley in the fold of the chalk downs.

PUB SIGN ▼

The tradition of hanging a sign outside an inn goes back to the first hostelries, the oldest of which is Ye Olde Trip to Jerusalem below the castle in Nottingham which dates back to the Crusades. Many pub signs recognise monarchs, local gentry or lauded personages; local 'sports' such as cock-fighting and bull baiting; while others refer to rural life and occupations.

VILLAGE GREEN ▼

Few things are more evocative of rural life than the village green, the traditional site for fêtes and celebrations like that at West Burton (Yorkshire Dales). Often with a pond, they were common land for grazing cattle and unhindered lawful sport and recreation, the latter freedom embodied within present-day legislation, the site for many cricket matches.

Cricket on the green, Lyndhurst, Hampshire

DRINKING FOUNTAIN ▼

Mains water supplies did not reach some households until the 1950s and villagers had to rely on communal springs, wells and pumps. During the 19th century, many towns and villages installed public drinking fountains like that at Langcliffe (Yorkshire Dales), but sadly most of these have disappeared or no longer work, to the disappointment of many a thirsty walker.

Dufton, Cumbria ©DK

◄ MARKET CROSS

Ranging from a simple stone shaft like that at Appleby-in-Westmorland to the elaborate shelter at Chichester (pictured), the market cross marked a place of gathering and the area set aside for the town's market. Styled on the churchyard crosses, where mass would be said as part of the Palm Sunday procession, they evolved into halls where trade was conducted like Somerset's butter market at Somerton and yarn market at Dunster.

STOCKS AND PILLORIES ▲

Medieval punishment was often summary and harsh, designed to inflict pain, humiliate and deter. Stocks hobbled the ankles with one- and two-ankle misdemeanours allowing at least three punishments to be administered simultaneously, whereas pillories secured neck and wrists, leaving the helpless prisoner vulnerable to the insults, rotten vegetables and often worse flung at them. Examples can be found at Stoke St Gregory (Somerset – stocks) and Nantwich (Cheshire – pillory). Their last reported use was at Newcastle Emlyn in Carmarthenshire in 1872.

LIGHTHOUSE ▶

In the days before telephone, radio and GPS, beacon fires served as warnings or to signal messages. The inaugural Trinity House lighthouse was built at Lowestoft in 1609, although the Romans erected Britain's first dedicated light at Dover. The threat of the Armada gave rise to a chain of 'Beacon Hills'.

LOCK-UPS ▼

Like this one at Mells (Somerset), village lock-ups still survive. They served as overnight jails for drunks or malefactors pending appearance before the magistrate. Usually

built as a single cell and often circular or octagonal, they fell out of use after 1839 when local police stations incorporating their own holding cells were built.

DOVECOTE ▼

Dovecotes, such as at Aberdour Castle (Fife - pictured), were built by the lord of the manor, although minor gentry often incorporated smaller roosts within their barns and houses, and served to provide the

family with a ready source of fresh meat through the winter. However, they were a bane upon the peasantry, for it was upon their crops that the pigeons fed.

◀ TITHE BARN

Medieval farmers were required to pay a tithe (or tenth) of their income to the church, usually rendered in the form of produce, which was stored in a large tithe barn close to the rectory. Abbey churches oversaw vast estates and consequently needed huge barns, often accommodating threshing floors as well. Fine examples can be seen at Bradford-on-Avon (Wiltshire – pictured) and Middle Littleton (Worcestershire).

Portland Bill, Dorset

FLINT MINE ▼

One of the earliest known industrial sites is Grimes Graves (EH, Norfolk) where flint (pictured) was mined on a massive scale over 5,000 years ago. The best nodules lay deep beneath the ground and were reached from vertical shafts. Hard and capable of being finely worked to a surgically sharp edge, flint was valuable and used for all manner of tools from axes to arrowheads.

©IS

QUARRY ▼

The Romans opened quarries to supply Hadrian's Wall as did the medieval cathedral and monastery builders. Like in mining, steam power and the refinement of explosives dramatically altered the industry, with huge quarries exploiting Welsh and Cumbrian slate, Dartmoor granite and Purbeck limestone (pictured - Winspit, Dorset). The limestone outcrops along the Pennines were quarried for lime and roadstone while in the North East, alum and ironstone were dug. Abandoned quarries are encountered in most areas, their faces often naturalised as cliffs, but a sure give-away is the flat floor footing the workings.

©MR

Hard Level Gill ©DK

©DK

Lead mine adit, Gunnerside, Yorkshire Dales

DRIFT MINE ▲

Prior to the industrial age, horizontal drift mining from adits and bell pits was common, serving local needs. Bell pits are evident in the Forest of Dean as collapsed hollows amongst the trees. Because of flooding and the difficulties of lifting material from great depths, deep mining only became possible with the invention of the steam engine.

©SFI

Carn Galver

◀ MINING ▲

The copper mines on the Great Orme (North Wales) were first worked around 2000BC and the Romans mined gold at Dolaucothi (Carmarthenshire). Tin, lead, iron and other metals were mined until the beginning of the 20th century, and abandoned sites such as the Carn Galver Mine (Cornwall) and the Hard Level Gill mines (Yorkshire Dales) indicate the extent of such industries.

LIMEKILN ▼

The practice of spreading lime on the fields was an 18th-century agricultural improvement and hundreds of limekilns sprang up around the countryside. Limestone burnt with coal produced quicklime, which when slaked, was used to counter the acidity of soil. During the 19th century, massive kilns like the ones at Froghall (at the terminus of the Caldon canal, Staffordshire) were built beside industrial quarries to produce lime for mortar and smelting iron ore.

Harkerside Moor, North Yorkshire

MILL CHIMNEY ▼

Towering mill chimneys, once common in industrial towns and cities, also rose singly in many secluded valleys where mills had originally been powered by water. An intriguing example is Lumbutts near Todmorden (Calderdale - pictured), where the steam engine replaced three waterwheels sited one above another.

Flatford Mill, Suffolk

WATERMILL ▲

During the Middle Ages, fast-flowing streams powered grist and fulling mills for flour and cloth production respectively. Watermills powered the first industrial processes such as iron making, textile production, wood turning and pin making. Aqueducts, weirs, leats and millponds helped with water management, while the development of reservoirs enabled ever-bigger mills. The tide mills at Eling, on the River Test where it flows into Southampton Water near Totton (Hampshire), and Woodbridge, on the River Deben (Suffolk), are the last surviving operational mills of their type.

Cley next the Sea, Norfolk

WINDMILL ▲

On hilltops and exposed sites windmills exploited the breeze to mill grain for flour. Other uses were developed and later, drainage mills powered by the wind were used for draining the fens of East Anglia and the Lancashire plain. There are three main types of windmill: post mill, where the body of the mill rotates around a vertical axis – High Salvington Mill, West Sussex; tower mill, now the most commonly seen, which has a rotating cap on top of a brick or stone tower – Cley windmill with its fan tail (pictured); smock mill, a lighter version of a tower mill usually built of wood – Union Mill, Cranbrook, Kent.

LOCK STAIRCASE ▶

Locks enable boats to pass up and down hill. A sequence of the familiar pound locks might be constructed to negotiate steeper or prolonged gradients. The flight of five locks at Bingley (West Yorkshire) has the steepest rise, while the thirty locks below Tardebigge near Bromsgrove (Worcestershire – pictured) form Britain's longest staircase.

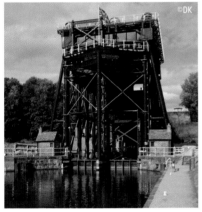

BOAT LIFT ▲

The extraordinary Anderton Boat Lift (Cheshire – pictured) and the iconic Falkirk Wheel (opened 2002) conserve water by using counterbalanced water tanks to transfer boats between two levels. Although no longer operational, the inclined plane at Blists Hill, Ironbridge (Shropshire) raised boats through 207 feet (63m).

WAGONWAY ▼

Britain's earliest wagonways were horse-drawn and served mines and quarries. The earliest recorded ones were developed in Nottinghamshire and Shropshire at the beginning of the 17th century and used wooden rails.

Greenhow Bank, North York Moors

AQUEDUCT ▼

Aqueducts carry a canal across a valley gap, bridging rivers and roads. Keeping them watertight posed considerable engineering problems and cast iron troughs were one answer. The Pontcysyllte Aqueduct (pictured) on the Llangollen Canal spans the Dee valley in north Wales, the highest (126 feet, 38m) and longest (1,000 feet, 305m) in Britain. It is a UNESCO World Heritage Site.

VIADUCT ▲

Little daunted Victorian engineers and the ¼-mile long Ribblehead Viaduct on the Settle-Carlisle line (pictured) has become an iconic memorial to the 1,000 navvies who spent four years building it. However, it was neither Britain's longest or highest, those accolades going to the Welland Viaduct - 1,275 yards (1,166m – Northamptonshire) and the now-demolished Crumlin Viaduct - 200 feet (61m – Caerphilly).

INDEX